Midnight Dreary

Midnight Dreary

The Mysterious Death of Edgar Allan Poe

John Evangelist Walsh

RUTGERS UNIVERSITY PRESS

New Brunswick, New Jersey and London

Second printing, 1999

Copyright © 1998 by John Evangelist Walsh
Manufactured in the United States of America

Library of Congress Cataloging-in-Publication Data

Walsh, John Evangelist, 1927–
Midnight dreary : the mysterious death of Edgar Allan Poe / by John
Evangelist Walsh.
p. cm.
Includes bibliographical references and index.
ISBN 0-8135-2605-1 (alk. paper)
1. Poe, Edgar Allan, 1809–1849—Death and burial. 2. Authors,
American—19th century—Biography. 3. Authors, American—19th
century—Death. I. Title.
PS2631.W28 1998
818'.309—dc21   98-24043
[B]   CIP

British Cataloging-in-Publication data for this book is available from the
British Library

Dedicated
as a welcoming bouquet
to my granddaughter
the sprightly

Katrina Marriott

who joined us on
19 May 1996

Contents

By Last Evening's Mail.

Death of Edgar A. Poe.

We regret to learn that Edgar A. Poe, Esq., the distinguished American poet, scholar and critic, died in this city yesterday morning, after an illness of four or five days. This announcement, coming so sudden and unexpected, will cause poignant regret among all who admire genius, and have sympathy for the frailties too often attending it. Mr. Poe, we believe, was a native of this State, though reared by a foster-father at Richmond, Va., where he lately spent some time on a visit. He was in the 38th of his age.—*Balt. Sun, 8th inst.*

Correspondence of the Baltimore Sun.

Arrival of the Falcon from Chagres, &c.

NEW ORLEANS, Oct. 5.

The news by the steamer Canada reached here last evening.

The steamship Ohio sailed for New York yesterday afternoon.

The steamer Falcon arrived here this morning. She was telegraphed at noon yesterday. The agent went in the Ohio to meet the Falcon and transfer the mails and passengers for New York. The Falcon is five days from Chagres to-day. She has fifty-nine passengers for New York.

There was no change in the cotton market yester-

Reprint in the Richmond *Republican*, October 9, 1849, of the Baltimore *Sun* story announcing Poe's death. The paper's editor deleted the word "year" from the last line to make the line fit. Poe was actually forty.

Prologue

The Case Reopened

t is a century and a half since the death of Edgar Allan Poe, and still there exist urgent questions about what happened, both circumstances and cause. In that situation, surely, there resides a macabre rightness. The man who invented the detective story, in his own sudden and bizarre demise, provided American literature with its most enduring real-life mystery.

The ingenious creator of the world's first consulting detective, Monsieur C. Auguste Dupin (from whom that parvenu Mr. Sherlock Holmes of Baker Street took his rise), in departing this life actually managed to do it in the best mystery-novel style. While traveling alone from Richmond, Virginia, to New York City, as if in a puff of smoke Poe disappeared from mortal view for nearly a week. When seen again after this lost interval he is found to be sodden with drink and tottering on the brink of the grave. Taken to a hospital, he is unable to say what happened to him, where he'd been all that time, who he'd been with. In another few days, after alternating periods of quiet and raving delirium, he dies. The immediate cause of death is given as "congestion of the brain," or "inflammation of the brain," serviceable phrases in a day that knew little of internal medicine.

In his own time and for decades later, no one seriously questioned the verdict that the culprit was liquor, that Poe died as a result of complications arising from a drunken debauch. As the immediate cause, some sort of physiological or orthostatic collapse was assumed, science in that day being unable to define it further. It was that conclusion which prevented the holding of a regular inquest on the body by city authorities—the drunkenness explained all, it was decided. Otherwise, since Poe had been found in extreme distress in a public place, that standard procedure would have been followed, and much more would now be known.

Inevitably, as the years passed and Poe's fame grew to world stature, efforts were made to clear him of what could only seem weak, wanton self-destruction. At least there was a hope that in some way his guilt might be lessened, and to that end various precipitating causes of a physical nature were suggested. On little or no evidence, a fatal heart condition of long standing was postulated, as was epilepsy, as well as a diabetic coma complicated by liver damage, and cerebral meningitis. Another idea conjured up a rare instance of *delirium tremens* being induced not by drink but by a severe toxic disorder, while another theory offered a blood deficiency, hypoglycemia. There was also an effort to put the primary blame on lawless thugs, either as robbers or as agents of election-day violence at the polls, the debauch following. Related to this last is a more recent suggestion that the cause of death was actually a brain hemorrhage brought on by some sort of head injury, perhaps a blow. As late as 1996 an article in the *Maryland Medical Journal* argued that the cause was really a case of rabies.

But none of this took permanent hold, and today the general belief as to the proximate cause of the final tragedy is pretty much what it was at the beginning. "Long-continued intoxication," one early memoir explained, was made sadly lethal by "a night of insanity and exposure." Even starker terms were used by another contemporary writer: "A day of wild debauchery" caused a fit of *delirium tremens,* "and he was taken out of the gutter by the watchman the next morning in a stupor." He'd simply indulged himself one time too many.

The missing piece of the puzzle, his whereabouts during the preceding several days, was in time quietly shrugged off. The most recent full-scale biography of Poe (1991), a volume massive and detailed, is content with merely stating that, aside from the drinking, "no reliable evidence exists about what happened." A 1996 reference work on Poe, the latest scholarly tool for study of his life and career, agrees, putting the fact more circumspectly: "The precise circumstances of his death were not then, and are not now, readily determined."

It was the passage of so much time that, predictably, dulled the topic, giving it that too-familiar feel which often overtakes old problems, no matter how urgent they once may have appeared. That it is not too late to bring it again to the forefront for one more try at a solution is my hope and my firm belief.

We are not primarily concerned here with the ever-vexed

question of the many-sided Poe character, its supposed defects and contradictions. Aside from one aspect of that character—his drinking—what manner of man he was is a subject mostly outside the present focus. But that single aspect, distasteful as it is, cannot be avoided in dealing with his death, raising anew the danger of a fatal distortion of the sort that has for so long roiled Poe's image, his reputation as a man.

Once for all, let it be stated that Poe was not a drunkard, not in the way usually meant by that term. Mostly, he was an exceptionally diligent and productive writer-editor, working in marvelously skillful fashion on both the journalistic and creative levels, a fact proved by the sheer volume, let alone quality, of his finished work. Terrible and disgusting enough when it did happen, his drinking came as a sudden interruption to that otherwise steady and sober existence (the current evolutionary phrase, "punctuated equilibrium," strikes me as exactly fitting the case).

As always with this type of alcoholism, the unsettling fact was its combined certainty and unpredictability. After long periods of perfect sobriety he seemed almost bound to fall again, and those who cared about him had to live with that relentless expectation. So much should be made clear before dealing with the circumstances of his death, for they tend to draw too sharp an emphasis on this weaker side, fixing on him the undeserved name of a thoroughgoing drunkard.

There is no doubt that Poe, when rescued in Baltimore, was far gone in a state of beastly intoxication. There is no doubt, or little doubt, that he had spent the previous night lying exposed in the open, too drunk to seek shelter. Equally certain is the fact that he had, just prior to being found, dropped out of sight, existing for days beyond any contact. It is precisely *that* undoubted fact which refuses to let the problem rest, in any event it does so for me, and I strongly suspect for a host of others. The sheer improbability of that sudden disappearance is what arrests the attention.

At that time, because of the great popularity of his poem *The Raven,* but also because of his remarkably varied tales, as well as his aggressive tactics as a critic, Poe's name was very well known to the public, his face less so (photographs, or daguerreotypes, had not yet reached the saturation point they eventually did, and few could be recognized by newspaper engravings). Indeed, in his final years he may have enjoyed the position of most famous American poet, taken solely as a matter of celebrity, if not most famous American author in general. How could the country's best-known poet and one of its leading writers, have so completely vanished from sight, gone missing, from midnight on September 26th, when he prepared to leave Richmond, to three o'clock on the afternoon of October 3rd, when he was picked up in Baltimore?

Convinced that an answer to that question *was* still possible, years ago I set myself to find it. Along the way that original interest spawned two other small books on Poe, neither of them concerned with his death but both in their own way works of investigation.* Whether I have in the present volume succeeded in my latest quest, whether the tantalizing mystery of Poe's demise may at last be taken off

---

* One of the two—*Poe the Detective*—was lucky enough to be awarded an Edgar by the Mystery Writers of America, bringing me a peculiar satisfaction: it was the first book about Poe to be given the award named in his honor.

the books as solved, is for the reader to decide (may I add that my own view is an emphatic thumbs-up!).

In these pages nothing has been merely imagined, no smallest item. Everything stated or suggested rests on authentic documents, and the narrative in that sense is a strictly factual one. I add what will be obvious from a glance at the extensive Notes section, that each step in the process is fully unveiled and explained (exhibits in evidence, we may say, laid out on a courtroom table).

In such a book as this—if ever!—the temptation is strong to quote from the tales in which Poe founded mystery fiction (*Murders in the Rue Morgue, Mystery of Marie Roget,* and *The Purloined Letter*). I must say I feel pleased with myself for being able, except in a single instance, to hold back. The sole exception I couldn't resist, it so exactly fits the uncovering of my pivotal clue. It will be found highlighted on the following leaf as epigraph.

Not the least usual error in investigations such as this is the limiting of inquiry to the immediate, with total disregard of collateral or surrounding events. . . . I would divert inquiry in the present case from the trodden and unfruitful ground of the event itself, to the contemporary circumstances which surround it. . . .

C. AUGUSTE DUPIN, IN
The Mystery of Marie Roget,
BY EDGAR ALLAN POE

Midnight Dreary

Once upon a midnight dreary, while I pondered, weak and weary,
Over many a quaint and curious volume of forgotten lore—
While I nodded, nearly napping, suddenly there came a tapping,
As of someone gently rapping . . .

FROM *The Raven,*
BY EDGAR ALLAN POE

₹ 1 ₹

Enter Poe

 *ts* broad, many-windowed facade topped by a large, square cupola from which flew a huge American flag, the recently completed American Hotel loomed grandly over Richmond's busy Main Street. An eye cast up and down the extensive, gently sloping thoroughfare would judge the American to be easily the most prominent building in sight.

On an oppressively hot morning in mid-July 1849 one of the city's regular horse-drawn omnibuses pulled to a stop before the American's front entrance, unexpectedly modest for so imposing a structure. As the compact little vehicle halted at the curb, its narrow rear door popped open and through it appeared a slightly built man, somber-faced and moving rather stiffly. Clutching a valise in one hand, he stepped down to the pavement, hurried up the stone steps,

I

and entered the hotel lobby. At the desk he signed the register, then accepted a key and climbed wearily up the stairs to his room.

Edgar Allan Poe, aged forty, and feeling a good deal under the weather, had arrived on stage for the final act of his often hectic personal drama. But of that sad fact he had no inkling. Despite a head still throbbing from a recent overindulgence, he had definite plans for the future.

Earlier that morning, after a journey of some thirty hours by train and steamboat, he had reached Richmond from Philadelphia, where he stopped over on his way south from his home in New York. The latter part of the journey had not been pleasant, for he was still feeling the effects of another of his prolonged drinking bouts, this one in the Quaker City, and in fact the worst yet. So extreme had been his intoxication in Philadelphia, where he lingered for two weeks, that he'd experienced his first full-blown fit of *delirium tremens,* complete with visions.

Taken briefly into police custody, he had escaped a formal charge, and jail time, through the accident of his being recognized by the judge. Only with the sympathetic help of some friends, including the gift of some cash to replace what he'd thrown away on liquor, had he been able to pull himself together sufficiently to continue his planned trip to the Virginia capital.

Secure at last in the quiet of his room at the American, he gratefully passed the remainder of the day resting, while duly applying whatever remedies and restoratives he'd come to depend on in these emergencies. Before approaching any of his friends in the city or getting in touch with those who were expecting him, he'd need time to bounce back. Miserable as he was in mind and body, his clothes also needing repair, he knew from experience with his previous sprees that a full recovery would be slow, requiring two or three whole days. He was not a man who held his liquor well.

Then, that same evening, real trouble showed up, posing a threat to his entire purpose in coming south. Taking his valise, he opened it and reached in for the manuscripts of two lectures he'd written especially for this trip. Rummaging through the folded clothes, collars, and personal items, he was alarmed to find that neither of the two manuscripts was in the bag. In Philadelphia the valise had reposed for days in storage at the railway station, and he now concluded that someone had opened the bag and stolen the lectures. Writing home later that evening in a mood of utter despair, he reported the shocking loss. "Think of the blow to me this evening," he lamented, "when on examining the valise, these lectures were gone. All my object here is over unless I can recover them or re-write one of them."

The lecture tour, scheduled for several other cities after Richmond, was not in itself the object or purpose of his trip. It was only the means to an end, one of considerable importance to him. The lectures would, he hoped, be the means of introducing to literate audiences the news of his projected new magazine, *The Stylus,* long dreamed of as taking rank with the leading American journals. Before any of the work on the magazine could be set in motion, editorial or otherwise, a list of one thousand firmly committed subscribers must be on hand, ensuring at least the cost of paper and printing for the first issue. That was the agreement he'd made with his financial backer, and if everything went as expected the plan was to have that first issue in the hands of readers by year's end or at least by January. It was a target date, as all those concerned in the risky venture were well aware, leaving precious little margin for delay.

At that moment in his room at the American, as the sounds of the darkening city drifted in with the suffocating heat through the open windows, the usually buoyant Poe had reached a very low ebb. "My clothes are so *horrible*," he added in a burst of remorse and yearning for sympathy as he concluded his letter, "and I am so *ill*."

Not really ill. That was just the way he and his family had learned to disguise the truth about his periodic binging, and the terrible debility that followed. But this time it was as much plain fear, desperate fear of another failure, that made him ill and made his clothes, wrinkled and stained as they may have been from his Philadelphia binge, appear so disgusting.

⁅ 2 ⁆

Enter the Widow

 *istant* only a leisurely stroll from the American Hotel, tucked into Richmond's eastern quarter, lay the city's Church Hill section, a comfortable enclave of old Virginia families. Through its middle ran East Grace Street, and at the juncture of Grace and Twenty-fifth, just opposite St. John's Episcopal Church, stood an aging but still elegant brick dwelling. Classically simple in line and proportion, it stood three stories high, with a lofty attic. The heavily paneled front door was daintily framed by a diminutive Greek revival porch, adding a touch of distinction to the frontage.

Here lived Elmira Shelton, aged thirty-nine, a widow with two children—Ann, aged nineteen, and Southall, aged ten. An active worshipper for many years at St. John's, Mrs. Shelton found her young life sadly disrupted five years before when she lost her husband to pneumonia. Even that untimely death was not the first or most grievous loss she'd had to endure. Her second daughter had died in infancy, as had a son born soon after, both cruelly taken off by disease.

As some compensation for the triple loss, poor enough in comparison, was the considerable fortune she had inherited from her husband. A prosperous merchant operating a line of freighters on the James River, as well as owner of a large carting firm, Alexander Shelton had become one of Richmond's wealthiest citizens. Exactly how much he'd left his wife isn't known but rumor at the time, apparently upheld by later reports, indicates that the figure could have been as much as a hundred thousand dollars (1849 dollars).

Trimly attractive, if no longer the full-lipped beauty she'd been in her youth, perhaps by now even a bit austere, Elmira had abundant dark hair and deep blue eyes that gazed steadily and knowingly on the world. Photographs made in her middle age show an unsmiling, even grim visage, an image that has misled many Poe biographers. As was often the case then, the unflattering pose was the photographer's fault. A closer, more lingering look at her old photos reveals a woman of somewhat patrician beauty, traces of what one old friend called her "lovely, almost saintly face."

Refined in manner, she spoke in a low, soft voice of singular sweetness, giving an impression slightly at odds with the reality. Neither shy nor retiring, she was well educated and was known for a certain force of personality. "Practical" was a word often used by her friends to describe her attitude toward matters of everyday.

Her marriage, which had lasted sixteen years at the death of her husband, from all that is known of it was a happy one. Yet in Elmira's background lurked one circumstance which may have brought into the Shelton home, now and then, a degree of real tension. Had it not been for the interference of her parents, more than twenty years before, Elmira would have married, not the well-to-do Mr. Shelton, but her next-door neighbor in Richmond, her earliest sweetheart, young Edgar Poe.

Almost since childhood, the two had known each other, and in 1826, on the eve of Poe's departure for the university, they had earnestly pledged their undying love and talked eagerly of marriage. Neither would become aware of it until much later, but not one of Poe's many ardent letters from school ever reached Elmira in Richmond. As each letter arrived it was quietly intercepted and destroyed by Elmira's father, who felt that his pretty daughter at age fifteen was far too young to be dreaming of a home and children of her own. During Poe's year away from home, neither received a single letter from the other, nor did either guess the real reason for the silence.

Over this part of the story there still hangs an obscuring cloud. No one can say just what happened between the two, only that the father's interference led to further misunderstanding. The unfortunate result was that Elmira, pressured by her parents, in December 1828 at age seventeen, became another man's wife. By then Poe had left home, later to join the army, and eventually pouring his heartbreak over Elmira into his first long poem, *Tamerlane*. His love for Elmira, he wrote in the extravagant fashion of young poets, was

> such as angel minds above
> Might envy—her young heart the shrine
> On which my ev'ry hope and thought
> Were incense . . .

and adding that even when skies were fair and life itself nothing but sunshine, "I saw no Heav'n, but in her eyes."

Another poem of the time written to his lost love, a brief lyric, seems to say that he attended, or at least saw her wedding. But that was poetic license, for on that catastrophic day he was nowhere near Richmond:

> I saw thee on thy bridal day,
>   When a burning blush came o'er thee,
> Though happiness around thee lay,
>   The world all love before thee:
>
> And in thine eye a kindling light
>   (Whatever it might be)
> Was all on earth my aching sight
>   Of Loveliness could see . . .

Were it not for one additional fact this tale of early love thwarted might be shrugged off as the usual excess of youthful ardor, an incident of no more than passing interest. But that sole fact by itself amply demonstrates quite the opposite, revealing the clinging anguish and lasting disappointment felt by Elmira over her girlish loss.

In 1836 Poe was back once more in Richmond, making a living as an editor of a magazine, *The Southern Literary Messenger.* In May of that year he was married to his cousin, Virginia. Soon afterward, while attending some social function never identified, Elmira unexpectedly encountered the new husband with his pretty bride on his arm. Her extreme reaction to that meeting seems to have surprised even herself, and some sign of her reaction must have been evident to Mr. and Mrs. Poe. "I shall never forget my feelings at the time," she later confessed, being careful not to say too much, but calling them "indescribable, almost agonizing." Though taken unaware by the meeting, she had bravely if with an effort recovered her composure: "in an instant I remembered that I was a married woman," and she banished the distressing memories "as I would a poisonous reptile."

That painful encounter was Elmira's last sight of the boy she'd loved. In the years since, she had settled into her comfortable niche as wife and mother, and mainstay of the Episcopal Church across the road. Poe, meantime, had gone on to literary renown, earning fame as critic, writer of strange tales, innovating journalist and, with publication of *The Raven* in 1845, taking rank as a celebrated poet, one much talked of, written about and endlessly praised.

The sudden tragic death of Elmira's husband in 1844 had brought no real change in the ordinary course of her existence. She was young enough to expect remarriage without delay, if she'd wanted it. But five years of widowhood, so far as is known, had produced no likely suitor, none at least who caught the fancy of the wealthy young matron. Increasingly, for whatever reason, her view of the future had become warily unsure and apprehensive. Less than a year before, in December 1848, in a letter to a favorite cousin, she had confessed her growing fear "that I shall never be a happy woman again." Avoiding specifics, she added the wan hope that time might accomplish "a great deal in obliterating past events from my feelings, but I am certain that I shall never feel like myself again."

Whether those "past events" included the heartbreak of her early romance cannot now be known. Little information as to the private life of this estimable woman during the intervening years of the 1830s and '40s is now recoverable. That was one of the unfortunate oversights of early Poe biography. Elmira Shelton lived on far past the time of the present discussion, and might have told much that is now lost.

Yet, as it turns out, the little that she did leave on the record, when studied minutely and in context—as up to now it has *not* been—proves just enough.

✿

Directly at the opposite end of town from the Shelton residence, also on Grace Street but almost in the suburbs, stood the squat, wood-frame home of the Talley family. Among the daughters of this house was a winsome, precocious young woman of eighteen named Susan, a budding poet aquiver with dreams of literary fame. A few of her poems had already appeared in some of the leading magazines, and had even won inclusion in the important 1848 volume, *The Female Poets of America,* edited by Rufus Griswold. More recently, word had reached her by winding ways that the great critic Poe himself, in correspondence with the editor of the *Messenger,* published right there in Richmond, had actually predicted that one day she would stand at the head of American women poets. Then she found that Poe had even put his opinion into print, in a review of the *Female Poets* volume. Miss Talley, he'd written, "ranks already with the best of American poetesses, and in time will surpass them all." Of course, he did add the sobering comment that her work exhibited some youthful defects "of experience and excessive sensibility, betraying her unconsciously into imitation." But then he'd closed his comment on her by stating roundly that she possessed "unmistakeable genius."

The fact that Mr. Poe was the only one who thought so highly of her work, the only one who would ever think so, or who would give her verse more than passing notice, hardly mattered. As she herself proudly recorded, Susan Talley was one of Poe's literary progeny, one of his earliest fans, awakened by him to literature's true power and glory. When hardly more than a girl, as she said, she had envisioned him as "a mysterious being in human shape, yet gifted with a power more than human; something of weird beauty and despairing sadness touched with a vague suspicion of evil, which inspired in me a sense of dread, mixed with compassion." When in July 1849 she heard that Poe was actually at that moment in Richmond, and that she would be introduced to him, she could hardly believe it: "I regarded the meeting with an eager, yet shrinking anticipation."

Only a few doors from the Talley home, further along on the same street, stood Duncan Lodge, impressive seat of the MacKenzie clan. In this house lived Rosalie Poe, younger sister of Edgar, adopted by the MacKenzies in her infancy. A plain, down-to-earth, naive woman with none of her brother's mental capacity (she may have been slightly retarded), Rose was some twenty years older than Susan Talley. But as the great poet's sister she exerted on her susceptible young neighbor a definite fascination, and the two had long been friendly. Finally, on a day in late July 1849, the eager Susan was afforded the thrill of a lifetime when an effusive Rosalie ushered her brother—after some days' rest feeling himself fully recovered from his Philadelphia indulgence—into the Talley home. Conducted by a servant, probably a slave, into the parlor, the two took seats and waited.

"As I entered the room" wrote Susan later, "Poe was seated near an open window quietly conversing. His attitude was easy and graceful, with one arm lightly resting upon the back of his chair. His dark curling hair was thrown back from his forehead, a style in which he habitually wore it. At sight of him the impression produced upon me was of a refined, high-bred and chivalrous gentleman."

Seeing Susan enter, Poe rose and "stood with one hand resting on the back of his chair," as he calmly awaited his young hostess' greeting. But he stood there so unexpectedly "dignified" in manner and attitude, "so reserved his expression," that the nervous Susan became thoroughly intimidated. She felt, as she described it, "an involuntary recoil" at what seemed a curious coldness (Poe may not have been warned that the young lady had been almost totally deaf from childhood and was all too conscious of her handicap). It was only a brief reaction, however, for the charm of the Poe personality soon asserted itself. Tentatively offering her hand, Susan was relieved to see the intense, dark eyes "suddenly brighten," and as her outstretched fingers were captured by her guest's welcoming grasp "a barrier seemed to melt between us."

From that memorable day Susan saw a great deal of the poet, either during his frequent stays at Duncan Lodge or in his many visits to her own home, where Susan and her family made him warmly welcome. Invariably she found him to be "pre-eminently a gentleman . . . dressed always in black and with faultless taste and simplicity. An indescribable refinement pervaded all that he said or did. His general bearing in society, especially toward strangers, was quiet, dignified, and somewhat reserved, even at times unconsciously approaching *hauteur*. He rarely smiled and never laughed."

Yet he was not quite the "melancholy person" Susan had expected. His mood among friends was invariably relaxed and cheerful. Often he would sit for hours surrounded by young people, listening in quiet amusement to their banter, now and then offering comments of his own, "humorous repartee tinged with playful sarcasm."

The visits to Duncan Lodge and the Talley home were the first that Poe paid after his arrival in Richmond. In the following two or three days he crowded in calls at the homes of many other old friends and acquaintances surviving from his own youth in the city. But very quickly—probably by the morning of Sunday, July 22nd, and in any case no later than the next Sunday—he found himself in the Church Hill section, mounting the steps of the little Greek revival porch at 2407 East Grace Street. Never before had he been to this house. Mrs. Shelton herself he had not seen in almost fifteen years. But this was the one place in Richmond he had for many months thought about visiting. Over and over in his mind he had pictured the details of what promised to be an emotional encounter, minutely rehearsing his own part in it.

That morning Elmira as usual was up early preparing for church. As she bustled about, a servant came upstairs to knock at her door and announce that there was "a gentleman in the parlor" asking to see her. Surprised at a call so early on a Sunday, wondering who the gentleman could be, she went down and was more than mildly taken aback to see her old love rising from his chair at her entrance. Her own all-too-brief description of the moment was given many years later. "I went down," she said, "and was amazed to see him—but knew him instantly. He came up to me in the most enthusiastic manner and said, 'Oh! Elmira, is this you!'"

Her personal reaction to the sight that greeted her so unexpectedly she never recorded further, only saying that after some minutes of welcoming talk, she took her leave. She was indeed very sorry, she told Poe apologetically, but she had been on her way out the door to church, and she "never let anything interfere with that." She'd have to leave immediately and hurry across the street or she would be late. But Edgar must call again very soon, she insisted, as soon as he could manage it. With that she departed, Poe no doubt leaving the house at the same time.

The abrupt termination of the long-awaited encounter would have left Poe in some little confusion, disappointed at finding that his presence was insufficient to alter Elmira's household routine. Perhaps he awoke to his mistake in choosing a Sunday morning to make his initial call. Perhaps he was also quick enough to catch what was probably the fact: that Elmira had simply used the handy excuse of church to make a temporary escape from a situation in which she found herself at something of a loss. Not wanting to put a foot wrong, she fled.

Poe's arrival at the house of his old flame may have been unannounced, and certainly the sight of him that particular morning took the lady unawares. But his appearance on the scene was by no means wholly unexpected. Long before this, Elmira had heard the news that Poe himself had become a widower, losing his young wife to consumption in January 1847. Almost inevitably, perhaps, she had begun to dream of a renewal of the old romance, now involving not a penniless boy and a slip of a girl, but a famous author (still nearly penniless!), and a socially prominent, very wealthy woman.

She didn't merely dream. By means of some casual comments dropped here and there among people she could expect to be in touch with the poet, she had sent subtle word of her interest in seeing him, cordial inquiries as to his health and well-being. One of these intermediaries, well chosen indeed, was John MacKenzie, adoptive father of Rosalie, who with his wife dutifully sent on to Poe at his home in New York, Elmira's best remembrances. On his own, MacKenzie then went further, urging Poe to think well and seriously about a marriage—a possibility that had occurred to any number of old Richmond residents who'd heard the pathetic story of the intercepted letters.

Considering everything, at that moment nothing could have seemed more natural or more in order than a match between the two former lovers. Elmira's money, some small part of it, could easily sustain the new magazine in its shaky beginnings. In turn, she would gain, in addition to belated fulfillment of her early romantic hopes, an enviable position in the then volatile field of American letters. Backer of the country's most important and influential journal (that was the hope), she would also take station as the wife of its brilliant editor.

Elmira's invitation for Poe to call again at the Grace Street house was quickly accepted, though just here no clue tells when, or how often, those subsequent meetings occurred, or what transpired. The little that is known was put guardedly on record by Elmira herself some twenty-five years later. Her own part in the renewal she deftly veils, summing up in a few short sentences what must have been a delicate courtship lasting perhaps three weeks:

"When he did call again he renewed his addresses. I laughed at it, [but] he looked very serious and said he was in earnest and had been thinking about it for a long time.

Then I found out that he was very serious and I became serious. I told him that if he would not take a positive denial he must give me time to consider of it. He said a love that hesitated was not a love for him. But he sat there a long time and was very pleasant and cheerful. He continued to visit me frequently . . ."

How she "found out" that Poe was indeed serious it would be interesting to know. Perhaps she meant simply that he convinced her by his earnest manner—the next sentence in any case shows her in a revealingly coy if not precious mood. Telling an ardent suitor that if he won't accept a *no,* then you are willing to reconsider, doesn't make much sense in that situation. Poe's own light remark in reply shows that he had already sensed the woman's quiet approval of the idea, and shows as well that he was enjoying the game.

If Elmira needed any reassurance as to her prospective husband's literary standing, she received it amply in his first lecture, given on the evening of Friday, August 17th in the large concert room of the Exchange Hotel. The supposedly lost manuscripts for the lecture, one at least, the principal one, had gratefully surfaced from some obscure corner of his belongings. Perhaps it had been rolled up in one of his shoes, stored in the small traveling trunk he is known to have had with him: a similar incident had happened at an earlier lecture in Boston, where panic over a missing manuscript had been calmed when he found the thin packet tucked into an extra pair of boots.

The audience that turned out for the lecture—a discussion of *The Poetic Principle,* as it was billed—drawn by advance publicity in several newspapers, was a large one, filling the hall. On the platform Poe stood "in a graceful attitude, leaning one hand on a small table beside him." Alternating comment and criticism with recitation of a series of shorter poems, his clear, rather musical voice "speedily brought the audience under its spell." He had no intention that evening, he began, to be either thorough or profound. While discussing more or less at random what it was that made poetry poetry, he would cite some "minor" verse as examples. As it developed, during the ninety-minute talk half the time was given to the recitation of verse, the rest to relaxed exposition.

Beginning with Shelley's *Indian Serenade,* he went on to read samples from three Americans (Willis, Longfellow, and Pinckney), and five more Englishmen (Moore, Hood, Byron, Tennyson, and Motherwell). Conspicuous in the front row sat Elmira, receiving, it is said, more than one caressing glance from the speaker. No record specifies it, but surely during his recitation of Pinckney's *A Health* he let his eyes stray down to linger on her upturned face:

> I fill this cup to one made up
>   Of loveliness alone,
> A woman, of her gentle sex
>   The seeming paragon;
> To whom the better elements
>   And kindly stars have given
> A form so fair that, like the air,
>   'Tis less of earth than heaven . . .

Cleverest and most effective of the selections, for purposes of a lecture, were those by Willis and Motherwell. The first served to perk his listeners up at the start, the second sent them out of the hall to a rousing finale. The

Willis piece (beginning "The Shadows lay along Broadway"), really had no business to be in the company of the other distinguished names, but it was at least clever, and it had considerable shock value. Openly it dealt with the question of prostitution in New York, and called for a more sympathetic understanding of such fallen women by the public ("the sin forgiven by Christ in Heaven / By man is cursed alway!").

The short Motherwell quote, only twelve lines, would have been spoken by Poe with all the verve he could muster. Before starting he observed that "with our modern and altogether rational ideas of the absurdity and impiety of warfare, we are not precisely in the frame of mind best adapted to sympathize with the sentiments, and thus to appreciate the real excellence of the poem. To do this fully we must identify ourselves with the soul of the old cavalier." Turning to his manuscript, his voice took on a dramatic urgency:

> Then mounte! then mounte! brave gallants all,
>   And don your helmets amain:
> Death's couriers, Fame and Honor, call
>   Us to the field againe.
> No shrewish tears shall fill our eye
>   When the sword-hilt's in our hand;
> Heart-whole we'll part and no whit sigh
>   For the fairest in the land;
> Let piping swain and craven wight
>   Thus weep and puling crye—
> Our business is like men to fight,
>   And hero-like to die!

Even that was not the end. As promised in the advance publicity, after the applause had died down, it was announced that Mr. Poe would recite his own wonderful composition, *The Raven,* which he did to great effect.

In the audience was Susan Talley and as Poe descended the platform to renewed applause, she recalled, the people, most of them strangely stirred, "arose, but made no move to retire, watching him as he talked and evidently waiting to speak to him." Rosalie Poe, hovering beside her adored brother, whispered to him excitedly, "Edgar, only see how the people are staring at the poet and his sister!"

Within a day or two appeared a number of newspaper reviews of the performance, and they said all that the speaker could have desired. "We were never more delighted in our lives," admitted the Richmond *Whig,* a sentiment echoed by the *Daily Republican,* which called the lecture "one of the richest intellectual treats we have ever had the good fortune to hear." The *Examiner,* equally full of praise, saw the speaker as "a man of very decided genius. Indeed we know of no other writer in the United States who has half the chance to be remembered in literary history."

Only about Poe's reading technique was there any slight demur. The *Examiner* editor, John Daniel, who was personally acquainted with the poet, complained that "his voice is soft and distinct, but neither clear nor sonorous. He does not make rhyme effective; he reads all verse like blank verse, and yet he gives it a sing-song of its own more monotonous than any versification. . . . He did not make his own *Raven* an effective piece of reading."

Some others concurred about the sing-song observation, finding an overemphasis on rhythm, and too much slurring of the rhyme. Yet there were many who reacted quite differently to the reading style, who felt, and said so forcefully, that Poe's readings were the grandest possible, nothing short of "soul-inspiring." In any case all were united in voicing the hope that so attractive and learned a personality would "make one more representation before us."

A month after his weary and despondent arrival in the city he again stood bravely atop the heights.

❦ 3 ❧

"We Regret to Learn . . ."

*n* the afternoon of Sunday, August 27th, ten days after his lecture triumph, Poe did something he would ordinarily never have dreamed of doing. Openly, almost ostentatiously, he joined a Richmond temperance society, publically swearing never again to touch liquor. At a regular meeting of the Sons of Temperance, Shockoe Hill Division, he held up his right hand, solemnly repeated the few words of the pledge, then signed a formal declaration to the same effect.

That date, and that curious event, together provide the sole certain facts by which a crucial question may be resolved: How long did Elmira take to "consider of" Poe's marriage proposal? When did she finally say yes?

The answer, obvious and firm, is reached by linking together several other undisputed facts. Within a matter of days of taking the pledge, Poe purchased a wedding ring, and then went out shopping for "a dress coat." In another day or two, writing home, he cheerily remarked that "the report of my intended marriage" had brought from his friends, the MacKenzies, greatly increased attention. He also about this time checked out of the expensive American Hotel and moved to the older Swan Tavern in Broad Street. A long, low-roofed structure with a railed porch decorating its front, the Swan was still quite reputable, comfortable in an old-fashioned way, but considerably cheaper.

Poe's surprising action in joining the cold-water army, and so conspicuously, caught the attention of others well beyond his own Richmond circle. On August 31st the movement's own newspaper, *The Banner of Temperance,* happily announced the new member. "It will be gratifying to the Sons of Temperance," said the paper, "to know that a gentleman of Mr. Poe's talents and attainments has enlisted in the cause." The story was picked up by many other papers in Virginia and surrounding states.

It was Susan Talley who put on record the fact that Poe, during his first weeks in Richmond, had proved unable to keep away from the bottle—not surprising in view of the "southern conviviality" he met on all sides, especially during his working visits to various newspaper and magazine offices, or while lunching with his journalistic brethren. As she heard it at the time, there occurred at least two drinking episodes, one apparently of short duration and of the milder sort as to quantity, the other more serious. Even if neither had been a true debauch, there would have been some days wasted in recuperation, and word of this inevitably reached Elmira.

No document actually connects Poe's taking the pledge with these latest incidents, no document suggests that his joining the temperance brotherhood was a condition imposed by the lady. But the linkage and progression are inescapable. While courting his widow, Poe gives way to his old enemy, upon which he takes the pledge, holding up his hand at a regular meeting of the order and signing his name to a formal declaration of reform, a printed card bearing his signature. Immediately there follows the widow's acceptance of the marriage proposal, and out he goes to buy a wedding ring and proper attire.

Elmira, it seems, had not needed all that much time to do her considering, a week at most, say, perhaps only days.

For decades it has been the fashion to belittle the romantic renewal of these two, especially decrying Poe's part in it as entirely mercenary. One of his most sympathetic biographers could see "no great rapture in this mature love story," but only a rather stark and pitiful "clutching at the memories of youth," and on Poe's part, "a desire to use her property" as underpinning for his new magazine. But it really appears to have been much more than that, at least in the end. Close familiarity with all the surrounding circumstances, and with one indisputable fact in particular, amply demonstrates that much of their old love had blossomed again, flourishing in a way that may have taken both by surprise. In marrying again, by the terms of her husband's will Elmira would lose most of her fortune, yet that fact failed to drive away the thought of marriage. This crucial information she must at some point have confided to her suitor, yet here again the dismaying news didn't turn him from his purpose. (Elmira would get only a fourth of the income she'd been used to receiving. The principal would be wholly taken out of her hands as executrix, and held in trust for her children.)

At the start, before the two had met again in Richmond, each had been rather deliberate about the situation, even somewhat designing. But their first weeks together, it seems, had changed all that. Before either quite realized it, perhaps, they had fallen in love all over again, their affection actually made stronger by virtue of their increased maturity. In a letter written immediately after Poe's death occurs the only outright statement Elmira would ever put on paper about her private feelings, but it is enough. In piercing anguish, she writes, "He was the *dearest object* on earth to me!" and asks helplessly, "How can I bear the separation!"

Poe's own deepest feelings are also clearly on record. After spending the evening of September 17th at Elmira's house, he confesses how much he has been stirred by her response to him. "I think she loves me more devotedly than any one I ever knew," he writes, showing some slight surprise at the unexpected turn of events, "& I cannot help loving her in return."

Word of the engagement was promptly written home by Poe to his mother-in-law in New York, Mrs. Clemm. Dependent on her son-in-law as she was, Mrs. Clemm would make a necessary part of the new household, a fact well understood and accepted by Elmira, and which caused her not the least concern. Knowing, however, that there might be some understandable apprehension on the point, she took an early opportunity of reassuring Mrs. Clemm directly, as to her own feelings, writing her a friendly and inviting letter after a Saturday evening spent with Poe in her parlor. At about eleven p.m., after Poe had departed, she went to her desk, picked up a pen and in the soft glow of an oil lamp wrote:

My Dear Mrs. Clemm,

You will no doubt be much surprised to receive a letter from one whom you have never seen. Although I feel as if I were writing to one whom I love very devotedly, and whom to *know* is to *love*—Mr. Poe has been very solicitous that I should write you, and I do assure you, it is with emotions of pleasure that I now do so—I am fully prepared to *love* you, and I do sincerely hope that our spirits may be congenial. There shall be nothing wanting on my part to make them so.

I have just spent a very happy evening with your dear Edgar, and I know it will be gratifying for you to know that he is all that you could desire him to be, sober, temperate, moral, & much beloved—He showed me a letter of yours in which you spoke affectionately of me, and for which I feel very much gratified and complimented. . . .

She reported that Edgar's recent lecture had been "very beautiful," had enjoyed a "very fashionable audience," and would be repeated shortly. She invited "her dear friend" to write to her in return, then she mentioned that the clock in the parlor had just struck midnight. "I am encroaching on the sabbath," she explained, "and must therefore conclude." To this pleasant missive Mrs. Clemm had replied promptly, expressing her own joy at the match. As reported by Poe, the return note brought from Elmira the glad comment that "it is such a darling precious letter that she loves you for it already."

Plans for the wedding had now been made firm, and a date chosen, October 17th. Since both bride and groom wished to have Mrs. Clemm present at the ceremony, and because there were some other small matters to be cleaned up, it was decided that Poe would go back to New York, conclude his business and bring Mrs. Clemm down with him. One other circumstance dictated a personal trip north, an editorial commission recently received from the wealthy husband of an ambitious poetess.

For a rather large fee of a hundred dollars, Poe was expected to "edit" the woman's verse for book publication (silently improve it in versification and diction), and also to make sure that her book when published would not be entirely ignored by the critics (a favorable notice from him was an unspoken part of the bargain). The poetess was Mrs. St. Leon Loud, and since she was a published writer, Poe could expect, at least, that her work would not be a complete embarrassment to him. She lived in Philadelphia, which lay conveniently on his route to New York from Richmond. The "editing" of the woman's manuscript, he expected, would occupy no more than a couple of days—for a hundred dollars he could scarcely give less.

Poe would leave Richmond, it was agreed with Elmira, the day after his second platform appearance, scheduled for Monday, September 24th, again at the Exchange Hotel. In all, it was thought that he'd be gone for some two weeks. That would leave ample time, after his return with Mrs. Clemm, to make the necessary preparations for the wedding, to be held at St. John's, across the way from Elmira's house. For the breakfast following the ceremony all would repair back to the Shelton parlor. Then Edgar and Elmira would go off by themselves to enjoy a little honeymoon alone at her other house in the country, Mrs. Clemm remaining at the Grace Street residence. Where the couple might finally settle for good was left open, although Richmond seemed an obvious choice.

It all made a very pleasant picture for those concerned,

and gave promise of a rosy future. Indeed, had it not been for one disagreeable circumstance, Poe's romantic return to the city of his youth, with its almost fairy-tale ending, would have been nearly idyllic. But that lone circumstance was enough to mar the portrait: neither of Elmira's children, Ann and Southall, was at all pleased at the prospect of having a new father in their house, and they didn't try to hide their feelings. In later years, Ann confessed to her own daughter that when Poe came to the house on Grace Street, her brother "would mimic the caller behind his back," while she, older by nine years, "giggling, would reprimand him." Both children, she added, took every chance of "discrediting the suitor in their mother's eyes." When at last the date was set for the wedding, both children "wept and pleaded with their mother not to marry Mr. Poe."

Less well attested in the documents, though undoubted, and equally or even more disturbing, was the opposition arising from another quarter, Elmira's relatives, of whom there were many in Richmond. This opposition, rather surprising in the circumstances, could have had only one cause: rumors about Poe's questionable reputation catching up with him, especially where women were concerned. No particular evidence is needed to support that assertion, for even in the normal course any number of revealing tales about Poe and women would have filtered through to Richmond, by way of newspaper reports full of innuendo, through the journalistic grapevine, and in private correspondence. What the rumors said about Poe's character, personal and literary, could not have been encouraging to anyone unblinded by personal motives. One of the most telling short descriptions of that character, written within months of Poe's death, shows how he was regarded by many observers up north (setting aside for the moment the degree of truth involved). "I knew something of Poe," wrote Walter Colton, "something of the unfathomed gulfs of darkness out of which the lightning of his genius sent its scorching flashes." For many people at the time, the phrase *gulfs of darkness* did not seem like much of an exaggeration when applied to Poe.

Either printed or circulated by word of mouth, the stories linked him in one way or another with no less than seven or eight women, all of them either married or widowed, all up north. Most damaging—and almost chillingly relevant to Elmira's situation—was a regrettable episode that had occurred less than a year before, when Poe had actually come within days of marrying another affluent widow, Sarah Helen Whitman, the Providence poetess. Rumor had it that Poe deliberately and cruelly broke the engagement when Mrs. Whitman, at the urging of her mother, arranged for a lawyer to put her money legally beyond the reach of a husband. Poe, it was claimed, had invaded the Whitman home while roaring drunk, knowing that such an exhibition would bring an abrupt halt to their intimacy. It had done just that, leaving a shocked and distraught Sarah stretched on a couch, her face buried in an ether-soaked handkerchief. (The truth of the matter seems not to have been quite so horrendous, though even today, with much more documentation available, it is difficult to sort out what happened in Providence in December 1848.)

Among the half-dozen or so other women named in the floating rumors was another poetess, the well-known Fanny Osgood, then estranged from her husband. Poe's connection with her had begun with several critical notices of her poetry, in which he badly lost his professional footing, stumbling into egregious over-praise. Fanny he found to be in many ways "without a rival," where in reality she was hardly more than a facile versifier of commonplace sentiment, barely above the level of the many rhymesters who supplied the day's newspaper and magazine verse.

Talk of the dalliance between the two, in New York City during 1845–46, would have been even more damaging than the Whitman scandal, for their affair had been conducted more or less in public, and included dark whispers about an illegitimate child. (The child was real, Fanny Fay, born June 1846. In some way impaired at birth, the baby lived only sixteen months.) The two had written poems to each other, full of innuendo, many of them published almost as soon as written. Also known was the fact that they were frequently together, several times meeting in places outside New York. Most notoriously, they had been together in Providence in October 1845, nine months before the birth of little Fanny Fay.

Most public of all Poe's prior female embroilments was the distasteful business of Mrs. Ellet's letters. Another New York City poetess of pedestrian talents, Elizabeth Ellet had formed a friendship with Poe, writing him frequently in unguarded fashion, of course hoping to win the critic more than the man. Eventually there was a falling out between them, and because of some slighting remarks by Poe about her letters, the woman's brother sent him a challenge. Incredulous, Poe refused a meeting on the field of honor over such a cause, and was informed by the brother that he would be the object of summary justice the first time they met in the street. To save himself from a public shooting, also to allay the almost hysterical fears of his sick wife, he was forced to send a written retraction and apology to the outraged woman. From New York City to Boston and beyond, the Ellet affair became the subject of wagging tongues.

How much of the detail of these and similar horrific tales may have reached Richmond, Elmira's relatives in particular, is hard to say. There was no lack of channels for such gossip, especially the network of journalists connected with newspapers and periodicals in and out of the city. John Daniel, outspoken editor of the Richmond *Examiner,* for instance, was well known at the north, acquainted with many writers in New York and New England, and was especially close to Mrs. Whitman. The same could be said for another prominent Richmond editor, John R. Thompson of the *Messenger,* as well as a large number of other reporters and writers. To one degree or another, journalists in general were fascinated by the Poe mystique and eager to gather news about him.

The really pertinent question is not how much did people in Richmond know about Poe. It is how much did Elmira know. Did her relatives ply her with damning information about her unstable fiancé, hoping to save her from what they saw as an utterly unpromising marriage to a predatory fortune hunter? That seems likely, to say no more. But then why didn't Elmira listen to them, heed their earnest warnings? For some readers the answer will be obvious, having to do with a woman's right in matters of the heart to believe what she wants to believe. Others will respond with a shrug, or with a puzzled shake of the head.

❧

Poe's second Richmond lecture was actually his third platform performance, for in mid-September he had gone downriver to speak at the old Norfolk Academy. That effort, said the Norfolk *Beacon,* had proved to be a delight for the eager audience, an ingenious display of poetic erudition "received with rounds of applause." Similarly, the *Argus* found the hour-long talk at the Academy to have been "chaste and classic . . . his recitations were exquisite, and elicited the warmest admiration." When, ten days later, Poe appeared at Richmond's Exchange Hotel his audience was the largest yet, numbering probably five hundred or more. With the price of the tickets set at fifty cents, and counting the fee from the Loud commission, Poe's financial worries were over for some months to come. His expenses for the journey north, and return, and for the wedding, would now be easily covered.

He didn't leave as planned the morning after the second Richmond lecture, however, probably because a note had reached him from Mrs. Loud asking for a short delay (he'd written her on the 18th asking for confirmation of the original appointment). That evening, the 25th, he spent with his sister at the Talley home, then went back to the MacKenzies', remaining there overnight. Next morning, the 26th, he went into town to see a variety of people on business, including John Thompson, whom he called on at the *Messenger* office. They arranged for some future contributions by Poe to the magazine, and Thompson made him a cash advance. Then, in strangely offhand fashion as he was leaving, Poe handed Thompson a small, rolled-up manuscript. "Here's a little trifle that may be worth something to you," he said casually. As Poe walked out, Thompson opened the thin roll to find a poem of six short stanzas. It began:

It was many and many a year ago,
    In a kingdom by the sea,
That a maiden there lived whom you may know
    By the name of Annabel Lee;
And this maiden she lived with no other thought
    Than to love and be loved by me.

I was a child and *she* was a child,
    In this kingdom by the sea;
But we loved with a love that was more than love—
    I and my Annabel Lee . . .

Thompson, knowing how Elmira and Poe had been torn apart in youth, could hardly have kept from linking the new poem—destined to take a place among the most exquisite American lyrics—and the old story. Whether the poem, in fact, was or was not written for and about Elmira remains a much harried question, but Poe's own motive in handing it to Thompson when and in the way he did is evident. He looked to have the new poem, so neatly, so precisely fitting the situation with Elmira, appear in the widely circulated pages of the *Messenger* as an accompaniment to the wedding. It would indeed have provided a superbly poetic comment on the renewed love affair, the perfect wedding gift for the bride.

On the evening of Wednesday, September 26th, Poe came to Elmira's house to take his leave of her. He would depart the city on the early morning steamer for Baltimore, where he would board the train for New York, stopping off briefly in Philadelphia. He might have taken the train the whole way, shortening the trip by several hours. But for no explained reason, on this first leg of the journey he preferred the slower, more roundabout means of the boat—chugging down the James River from Richmond, then a swing north up the long, wide stretch of Chesapeake Bay. He'd be in Baltimore on the morning of the 28th, and if he made his train connection would reach Philadelphia that same evening. After that, arrival by Sunday at his home in New York was a good possibility, but in any case by Monday, October 1st. More delay than that he couldn't well afford if things were to proceed smoothly.

Bidding him goodby, Elmira, as she stated afterward, thought he seemed "very sad." Poe himself, she said, admitted to feeling pretty sick, while mentioning nothing specific: "I felt his pulse and found he had considerable fever, and did not think it possible that he would be able to start in the morning." (How feeling a pulse revealed the presence of a fever isn't clear.) That night she felt "so wretched about him" that she hardly slept at all.

Still worried when she arose next morning, she had the buggy hitched up and then drove over to the Swan, hoping to find that Poe had postponed his departure. She was informed that he wasn't there, that he was on his way north: "much to my regret he had left in the boat for Baltimore."

The two had agreed that Poe would write to her the very day he reached home. That meant Elmira could expect to receive a letter in a week at the outside. But a week passed and no letter came, and thereafter each day that drifted by in silence heightened her concern. Slowly, September rolled into October while Elmira, hurrying her preparations for the wedding, counted each day of the new month.

On the morning of October 9th she picked up her usual copy of the Richmond *Daily Whig*. As she afterward stated, she was glancing casually over the close-printed

columns when her attention was caught by a mention of
Poe's name. At first, with her eyes speeding in sudden
fright along the lines of type, her racing mind wasn't quite
able to take in what it was reading:

> DEATH OF EDGAR A. POE.—We regret to learn that
> Edgar A. Poe, Esq., the distinguished American poet,
> scholar and critic, died in this city yesterday morning,
> after an illness of four or five days. This announcement,
> coming so sudden and unexpected, will cause poignant
> regret among all who admire genius, and have sympathy
> for the frailties too often attending it. Mr. Poe, we believe,
> was a native of this State, though reared by a foster-father
> at Richmond, Va., where he lately spent some time on a
> visit. He was in the 38th year of his age.

It took a few moments before Elmira realized that the
phrase "this city" didn't mean Richmond. The brief paragraph was a reprint from the previous day's Baltimore *Sun*.

On its own, the *Whig* added its "profound regret" at the
shocking news, but supplied no details as to cause or circumstance. Other Richmond papers proved equally bare of
additional facts, and it took the frantic Elmira two days to
get hold of some other Baltimore publications. There was
precious little added information in any of them, merely
that Poe had succumbed to "congestion of the brain."

Once convinced of the truth of the report (in those days
of more casual journalism, readers frequently doubted a
story's accuracy, often with good cause), Elmira poured her
shock and despair into a letter to Mrs. Clemm: "I cannot
begin to tell you what my feelings were as the horrible
truth forced itself upon me! It was the most severe trial I

have ever had, and God alone knows how I can bear it! My heart is overwhelmed—yes, ready to burst! Oh, my dear Edgar, shall I never behold your dear face & hear your sweet voice . . ."

As to the real cause of Poe's death, enough of a clue for most readers, Elmira included, was that veiled reference to the "frailties" of the artistic temperament. In the Baltimore *Evening Patriot* of the 9th, the catchword appeared again, in a passage lamenting how so admirable an author had been "obscured and crippled by the frailties and weaknesses" too often attending genius. No one reading those stark words needed to have it explained that a long-continued habit of drink, of pathetic, reeling drunkenness, had claimed another victim.

When her disbelieving eyes first fell on the *Whig's* stark notice, Elmira could not have guessed it, but at that moment Poe had been in his grave one entire day. In the Presbyterian Cemetery of Baltimore, at four o'clock on the afternoon of October 8th, a dark, raw, dismally wet day, the earth closed over all that was mortal of the man many people in sincere admiration had begun to call simply *The Raven.*

Huddled beneath umbrellas around the open grave as the coffin was lowered stood no more than a half-dozen mourners.

❴ 4 ❵

Witness Time

*uriously,* only one reporter in Baltimore in October 1849 bothered to make more than the usual perfunctory inquiry about the death of the famous poet. That was the anonymous correspondent of the New York *Herald,* who filed his copy from Baltimore on October 8th. Next day the story appeared in the paper on page three under the general heading, "Our Baltimore Correspondence." Mr. Poe, it said, had "arrived in this city about a week since," after a successful lecture tour in Virginia. Then, the story continued,

> On last Wednesday, election day, he was found near the Fourth ward polls laboring under an attack of *mania a potu,* and in a most shocking condition. Being recognized by some of our citizens, he was placed in a carriage and conveyed to the Washington Hospital, where every attention had been bestowed on him. He lingered, however,

until yesterday morning, when death put a period to his existence. He was an eccentric genius, with many friends and many foes, but all, I feel satisfied, will view with regret the sad fate of the poet and the critic.

Stating the facts as they would have struck the *Herald*'s readers, it seemed that Poe had been found extremely drunk in the street, raving insanely, and physically battered—or perhaps the "shocking condition" referred to the state of his clothing. Recognized by some passerby—or more than one—he was taken to a hospital. Despite the most unstinting medical care, he died in the hospital in a matter of days. Implied as the cause of death were undetermined complications from excessive liquor intake, perhaps made worse by exposure.

Very typical of the time was the absence in the *Herald* account of all the detail a modern reader would expect to find: dates, names, times, exact locations, some observations by the local police, and comment on the case by hospital authorities (the term *mania a potu,* better known as *delirium tremens,* may have been supplied by the doctors at the hospital). As it was, an interested reader of the *Herald* could, with a little effort, discover that Poe had been picked up on October 3rd, and had died on the morning of the 7th. When found he was "near" the polling place of the city's "Fourth ward," which meant a building called Gunner's Hall on Lombard Street, the actual polling site being in the hall at Ryan's Tavern (a "tavern" then was not a saloon, but was more like today's inn. At that time they were often used to house polling booths).

October 3rd was election day for representatives to the United States Congress, which accounts for the polling place being in operation. Poe's rescuers "recognized" him,

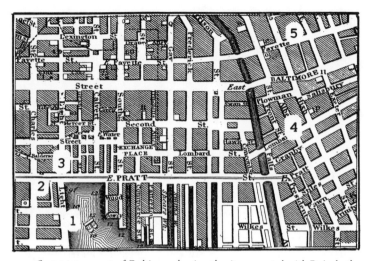

*Contemporary map of Baltimore showing the sites connected with Poe's death.
1) steamboat dock; 2) railway depot; 3) Bradshaw's Hotel; 4) Ryan's Tavern in
Gunner's Hall where Poe was found; 5) home of Dr. Snodgrass at 103 High Street.
Washington College Hospital, where Poe died, was a mile or so to the right along
Baltimore Street.*

wrote the *Herald* reporter, but that bit of information raises
more questions than it answers, for it was not a day when
celebrities could be spotted on sight as they are now. Photographs were not yet being published in magazines and
newspapers, only engravings made from them, and these
were not at all plentiful, nor always accurate. The odds
against *any* celebrity being recognized in public were great.
Add the fact that this particular celebrity was horribly in-
toxicated, was in a highly excited emotional state, was certainly disheveled, and was sitting or lying on the pavement
(this most readers would have assumed). The necessary conclusion is that whoever came to Poe's assistance was a friend
or at least a personal acquaintance.

With the appearance of the *Herald* story, though much
continued to be written about Poe in publications north

and south, attention to the circumstances of his death soon waned. In the following weeks or months no further details surfaced, nor did any investigator undertake to search for them. The Baltimore coroner, apparently not doubting the verdict of death by alcoholism, held no inquest on the body. Nor did the Baltimore police, so far as is known, feel any particular concern over the demise in their fair city of one of the country's leading literary men. All were satisfied, it seems, that the poet's untimely end was a direct result of his own willful act of debauchery. His dying alone and far from home—unfortunately in the gutter, was the thought of many readers—of course was a pity. But it all seemed so inevitable.

Behind the scenes, meanwhile, some others learned a bit more. An urgent note from Mrs. Clemm to a cousin of Poe's in Baltimore brought a quick if less than satisfactory answer. Neilson Poe, it developed, had visited the ailing man in the hospital. Since then he had been making inquiries but had turned up nothing new: "At what time he arrived in this city, where he spent the time he was here, or under what circumstances, I have been unable to ascertain. It appears that on Wednesday, he was seen and recognized at one of the places of election in old town, and that his condition was such as to render it necessary to send him to the college [Washington College Hospital]."

Overlooking such pertinent items as how and when he was alerted to his cousin's presence in the hospital, and who it was that told him, Neilson goes on to unfold his own brief part in the tragedy:

As soon as I heard that he was at the college, I went over, but his physicians did not think it advisable that I should see him, as he was very excitable—The next day I called and sent him some changes of linen, etc. and was gratified to learn that he was much better, & I was never so shocked in my life as when, on Sunday morning, notice was sent to me that he was dead. Mr. Herring and myself immediately took the necessary steps for his funeral, which took place on Monday afternoon at four o'clock. . . . If I had known where a letter would reach you I would have communicated the melancholy tidings in time to enable you to attend his funeral. . . .

Mr. Herring and myself have sought in vain for the trunk and clothes of Edgar. There is reason to believe that he was robbed of them whilst in such a condition as to render him insensible of his loss. . . .

He ends with profuse expressions of sympathy and regret ("Edgar had seen so much of sorrow"), but saying not a word more about the likelihood of Poe's having been robbed, or where in the city he and Mr. Herring (a Poe cousin) had sought for the dead man's "trunk and clothes."

Also readily responding to Mrs. Clemm's appeal for information was the doctor who attended him during those four nights in the hospital, John J. Moran, resident physician, as he styled himself. In penning his reply he took pains to say that he was drawing on his official notes, "the Records of the case." Lengthy and well-considered, his letter, which still exists, is dated November 15th, some five weeks after Poe's burial, and only one day after receiving Mrs. Clemm's inquiry. Its opening lines, mourning the loss of "this rarely gifted mind," show that the young doctor—he was only twenty-seven—had been keenly aware of his patient's identity ("How many thousands will yet, and for years to come, lament the premature demise of this truly great man!"). At last he gets down to medical matters, but then, to spare Mrs. Clemm's feelings, slides into his text in the most disappointing way, failing to specify the cause of death:

> Presuming you are already aware of the malady of which Mr Poe died I need only state concisely the particulars of his circumstances from his entrance until his decease—
>
> When brought to the hospital he was unconscious of his condition—who brought him or with whom he had been associating. He remained in this condition from 5 Ock. in the afternoon—the hour of his admission—until 3 next morning. This was on 3rd Oct.
>
> To this state succeeded tremor of the limbs, and at first a busy, but not violent or active delirium—constant talking—and vacant converse with spectral and imginary objects on the walls. His face was pale and his whole person drenched in perspiration. We were unable to induce tranquility before the second day after his admission.
>
> Having left orders with the nurses to that effect, I was summoned to his bedside so soon as consciousness supervened, and questioned him in reference to his family—place of residence—relatives etc. But his answers were incoherent & unsatisfactory. He told me, however, he had a wife in Richmond (which I have since learned was not the fact), that he did not know when he left that city or what had become of his trunk or clothing.

Hoping to "rally" his patient, and instill a more optimistic frame of mind in place of the gathering despair, Moran told him that he had every expectation that a very few days would see him on the mend and back in the bosom of his friends. Meantime, he added earnestly, everything possible was being done for his comfort and to speed his recovery:

At this he broke out with much energy and said the best thing his best friend could do would be to blow out his brains with a pistol—that when he beheld his degradation he was ready to sink in the earth, etc. Shortly after giving expression to these words Mr Poe seemed to dose & I left him for a short time.

When I returned I found him in a violent delirium, resisting the efforts of two nurses to keep him in bed. This state continued until Saturday evening (he was admitted on Wednesday) when he commenced calling for one "Reynolds," which he did through the night up to *three* on Sunday morning.

At this time a very decided change began to affect him. Having become enfeebled from exertion he became quiet and seemed to rest for a short time, then gently moving his head he said *"Lord help my poor soul"* and expired!

This, Madam, is as faithful an account as I am able to furnish. . . .

Closing, Moran assures his correspondent that the patient had "lacked for nothing" in the way of medical care, "Indeed we considered Mr Poe an object of unusual regard." Word of his presence had spread quickly through the hospital bringing many among its personnel to his bedside, doctors, nurses, clerks, and even students. All these visitors had spoken words of encouragement, and "sympathized earnestly with him." He has been so candid, adds Moran, because Mrs. Clemm asked it. Left to himself, he would never "even hint a fault of his."

Of course, Moran had not been as candid as he might and should have been. Addressing the dead man's family, he had no need to avoid stating clearly what he judged to be the true cause of death, only hinting at the drunkenness, and the case of severe *delirium tremens* that had his patient

Sarah Elmira Royster Shelton, in a photo made in her middle age, probably during the Civil War. The grim expression of her face belies the reality of her warm, sensitive nature and outgoing personality. (Valentine Museum, Richmond, Virginia)

The Richmond home of Mrs. Shelton at 2407 East Grace Street, in an early photograph. Still standing, the structure is virtually unchanged. Here Poe bade Elmira goodby the night he left Richmond. She never saw him again. (Valentine Museum, Richmond, Virginia)

Edgar Allan Poe in a daguerreotype made in Richmond in 1849, perhaps soon after his arrival in July (the Dimmock copy, Hampton-Booth Theatre Library, The Players Club, NYC). The moustache supplies peculiar evidence in the unfolding of the mystery.

Sketch of the teenaged Elmira Royster (Mrs. Shelton), supposedly made by Poe when the two became engaged in youth. It is almost certainly a modern fake. See "Added Note," p. 145. (Lilly Library)

Engagement gift of Poe to Elmira Shelton, containing a lock of his hair. Engraved on the lid are his and her initials. (Oliver R. Barrett Collection)

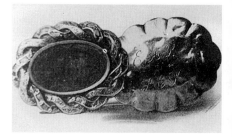

Above, left: *Susan Archer Talley (Mrs. Weiss). She saw much of Poe in Richmond before he departed on his fatal journey.* Above, right: *Maria Clemm, Poe's mother-in-law, who was also his aunt. Revering his memory, she outlived him by twenty years.* Below: *The Talley home in Richmond where Poe was many times a guest in the fall of 1849.*

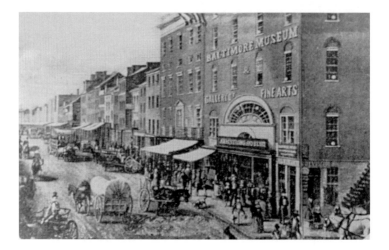

Above: *Baltimore 1849, corner of Calvert and Baltimore streets, near the Fourth Ward polls where Poe was found.* Below: *A frantic note from Mrs. Clemm to a Baltimore cousin asking confirmation of Poe's death.*

Dear Nelson

New York Oct 9

I have heard this moment of the death of my dear son Edgar — I cannot believe it, and have written to you, to try and ascertain the fact and particulars — he has been at the South for the last three months, and was on his way home — the paper states he died in Baltimore yesterday — If it is true God have mercy on me, for he was the last I had to cling to and love, will you write the instant you receive this, and relieve this dreadful uncertainty — My mind is prepared to hear all — conceal nothing from me.

Your afflicted friend

Maria Clemm

Presuming you are already aware of the malady of which
Mr. Poe died I need only state concisely the particulars of
his circumstances from his entrance until his decease –

    When brought to the Hospital he was unconscious of
his condition – who brought him or with whom he had been
associating. He remained in this condition from 5. Ock in
the afternoon – the hour of his admission – until 3 next morning.
This was on the 3rd Ock.

        To this state succeeded tremor of
of the limbs, and at first a busy, but not violent or active delirium – constant talking – and vacant converse with spectral
and imaginary objects on the walls. His face was pale and
his whole person drenched in perspiration – We were unable
to induce tranquility before the second day after his admission.

    Having left orders with the nurses to that effect, I was
summoned to his bedside so soon as consciousness supervened, and
questioned him in reference to his family – place of residence –
relatives &c. But his answers were incoherent & unsatisfactory.
He told me, however, he had a Wife in Richmond (which, I have
since learned was not the fact) that he did not know when
he left that City or what had become of his trunk of clothing.

    Wishing to rally and sustain his now fast sinking hopes
I told him I hoped, that in a few days he would be able to
enjoy the society of his friends here, and I would be most
happy to contribute in every possible way to his ease & comfort.
At this he broke out with much energy, and said the best
thing his best friend could do would be to blow out his
brains with a pistol – that when he beheld his degradation
he was ready to sink in the earth &c. Shortly after giving

Second page of Dr. Moran's three-page letter to Mrs. Clemm in which he details Poe's troubled last hours. "We were unable to induce tranquility before the second day," he explains in lines 13–14 (see Chapter Four for the remainder of the letter). Moran was the hospital's resident physician.

Above, left & right: *John Sartain and George Lippard, both of Philadelphia.* Right: *Mrs. Elizabeth Oakes Smith, of New York.* Below, left & right: *John R. Thompson, and John M. Daniel, both of Richmond.*

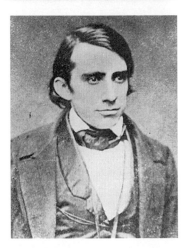

talking to "imaginary objects on the walls." Instead of making an outright declaration in writing, he presumed that Mrs. Clemm already knew the nature of the "malady."

Even so, the portrait Moran gives of Poe's final hours and minutes was harrowing enough, and must have brought considerable distress on poor Mrs. Clemm. Aside from that, he provided no new facts of any real substance, though he did manage to create a minor puzzle with his offhand reference to the "Reynolds" so loudly and lengthily invoked by Poe in the blur of his last night of life. The dead man had no relatives by that name, no friends or colleagues, so far as anyone knew.

Surprisingly—even, it can be said, incredibly—more than six years were to pass before a fuller picture of Poe's last days and hours became available. In May 1856, a New York City periodical, *Life Illustrated,* carried an article by Joseph Snodgrass of Baltimore, an old friend and journalistic colleague of the poet. It revealed Snodgrass to be the one who transported the inebriated Poe from tavern to hospital, and much else of interest besides.

Called to the tavern by a note from someone he fails to identify, Snodgrass walked into the establishment's barroom. Though warned that Poe was not in good condition, the sight of the poet sitting slumped in a chair left Snodgrass almost in shock. The face "wore an aspect of vacant stupidity which made me shudder. The intellectual flash of his eye had vanished, or rather had been quenched in the bowl." Snodgrass' astonished gaze next fell on the clothes, and again he was taken aback:

His hat—or rather the hat of somebody else, for he had evidently been robbed of his clothing, or cheated in an exchange—was a cheap palm-leaf one, without a band,

and soiled; his coat, of commonest alpaca, and evidently "second-hand"; and his pants of gray-mixed cassimere, dingy and badly fitting. He wore neither vest nor neck-cloth, if I remember aright, while his shirt was sadly crumpled and soiled. He was so utterly stupefied with liquor that I thought it best not to seek recognition, or conversation, especially as he was surrounded by a crowd of drinking men, actuated by idle curiosity rather than sympathy.

Nonplussed, trying to decide what to do, Snodgrass was about to engage one of the tavern's rooms as a temporary haven for his friend. But at that moment a relative of Poe's (unnamed, but later identified as Mr. Herring) walked in. Seeing him, Snodgrass assumed he would take Poe to his own home, and was quite surprised to hear Herring refuse. When drunk on a former occasion, Poe had been "very abu-sive and ungrateful" toward the members of his family, said Herring, and he would not take the chance of a repeat per-formance. The Washington Hospital, he finished, was the place for his troublesome relative. Snodgrass, glad to have the decision made for him, consented.

Lifting Poe to his feet, the two found that he couldn't walk, could hardly stand. "So insensible was he," recalled Snodgrass, "that we had to carry him to the carriage as if a corpse." From Poe, as the little group went clumsily out the tavern door, came "incoherent mutterings."

Obviously, Snodgrass had remembered Poe for what he ordinarily was, a very careful, neat dresser, not exactly fash-ionable but always well turned out, always conscious of his appearance. Yet here he was wearing a strange assortment of odds and ends: the cheapest sort of hat, damaged and soiled — trousers and coat (suit-jacket) of commonest make and fabric, both rumpled, the pants ill-fitting — no vest, in a time when every gentleman wore one, its absence disclosing a dirty shirt open at the neck, with no sign of a tie or neckcloth. At a loss to explain what he saw, Snodgrass can think only that Poe's attire seemed not his own. Second-hand, he guesses, in part anyway, and stops there.

Ten more years were to pass before Snodgrass offered anything further about his disagreeable errand that morning, this time in *Beadle's Monthly*. By then the event itself was nearly two decades old, and Snodgrass was falling into some obvious errors, dates and names mostly, and clearly as a result of not bothering to check. But he finally gave the name of the man who had first found Poe, and who had sent the initial note alerting Snodgrass to the emergency. The man was a Mr. Walker (no first name supplied), who had once worked for Snodgrass as a typesetter. No details of that first encounter between Walker and the poet are filled in, only that Poe had managed to mutter Snodgrass' name.

Again Poe is pictured sitting in a chair in the bar, stupefied by drink, "head dropped forward." The face Snodgrass saw was not only haggard, it was "bloated and unwashed," the dark hair unkempt, "his whole physique repulsive." The battered old palm-leaf hat, the cheap, ill-fitting clothes, the soiled shirt, all are detailed as before. To the list is added only one new item, "boots of coarse material, giving no sign of having been blacked in a long time."

Disappointingly, as was soon found, by then Mr. Walker had himself passed on, having died in a drowning accident in Baltimore's Spring Garden. It was not until after Snodgrass' own death, in 1880, that anyone realized that

Walker's original note had survived. Snodgrass' widow found it tucked away with other Poe things, the rather coarse paper somewhat damaged by damp, but the writing entirely legible. This crucial message entered the public record in March 1881 through the columns of the New York *Herald*:

Baltimore City, Oct 3d 1849

Dear Sir,—

There is a gentleman, rather the worse for wear, at Ryan's Fourth ward polls, who goes under the cognomen of Edgar A. Poe, and who appears in great distress, & he says he is acquainted with you, and I assure you, he is in need of immediate assistance.

Yours in haste,
Jos. W. Walker

To Dr. J. E. Snodgrass

Thus unexpectedly surfaced documentary proof for the repeated early assertion, first mentioned in October 1849 by the New York *Herald,* that Poe had been found at, near, or in one of the city's polling stations, and that the polls had been located at Ryan's Tavern (easily placed at Gunner's Hall in Lombard Street). The Walker note in addition, of course, afforded a peculiar satisfaction to the legion of Poe admirers, as well as biographers. Yet as it turned out it meant far more than that. Actually it was taken as lending final firm support to the only alternate theory of Poe's death to gain wide acceptance.

Before that track is followed, however, it is necessary to give another hearing to the physician who attended Poe's deathbed, Dr. John J. Moran. Now older by twenty-five

years, Moran had never been able to forget the part he had
played in the dramatic death of a great poet.

In a corner of the Presbyterian Cemetery in Baltimore in
the fall of 1875, a small crowd gathered to dedicate a
monument to Edgar Allan Poe, the city's first such recognition of him. Attending as an honored guest was Dr.
Moran, who had been asked to verify the date of Poe's
death. Until then completely absent from any direct hand
in Poe matters, the doctor found his old fascination with
the poet aroused by this widely reported ceremony, and
soon he had begun a second career as a lecturer on Poe.
Presenting himself as the principal witness of the dying
hours, he also supplied commentary on the life, and the
circumstances leading up to the tragedy.

The immediate impetus, perhaps, for Moran's sudden
blossoming as a Poe expert came from the attention ac-
corded him by newspaper accounts of the dedication, in
which he was quoted at length. They show him, even this
early, busily engaged in his self-appointed task of rescuing
the poet's reputation, which he began by simply contra-
dicting himself, blandly denying that alcohol had been
in any way involved. "He succumbed to an overdose of
opium," Moran is quoted as saying by the *Herald,* "which
he had taken to allay the excitement of his very sensitive
nervous system." It was a clumsy substitute for drink that
he offered, but more acceptable in that day, when lauda-
num, a combination of opium and alcohol, was freely available as a medicine, which is what Moran meant.

Presumably with a straight face, Moran added that there
was "no smell of liquor upon his person or breath. There

was no delirium or tremor." Instead, on the lips of the dying poet were mournful utterances about time and eternity, last words deemed suitable for a poet, but which must have brought from the *Herald* reporter a disbelieving smile ("Oh, God! is there no ransom for the deathless spirit!" etc.).

In 1885, Moran's oft-repeated lecture, considerably expanded, was published as a book, and for this Moran provided some new details concerning the final days and hours, even naming his source. Soon after Poe's death, he explained, a man named George Rollins, of Baltimore, stopped him on the street. Then employed as a train conductor, Rollins said he'd read of Poe's death in the papers, and had something to say that Moran might like to hear. In Baltimore, Rollins went on, Poe had boarded his train, headed for Philadelphia. But when the train reached the banks of the Susquehanna, where passengers switched to boats for the crossing to another train on the other side, Poe had stayed in his seat and had gone back to Baltimore. Rollins thought the reason for his not going on might have been the storm then raging, making the river very rough.

At some point during the return, added Rollins, two men looking like "sharks" had entered the coach and taken seats back of Poe. In Baltimore they'd gotten off when he did, and seemed to be following him. Here Moran picks up the thread:

> When he reached the southwest corner of Pratt and Light Streets he was seized by the two roughs, dragged into one of the many sinks of iniquity or gambling hells which lined the wharf. He was drugged, robbed, stripped of every vestige of clothing he had on . . . and reclothed with

a stained, faded old bombazine coat, pantaloons of a similar character, a pair of worn-out shoes run down at the
heels, and an old straw hat. Later in this cold October
night he was driven or thrown out of the den in a semi-
conscious state, and, feeling his way in the darkness, he
stumbled upon a skid or long wide board lying across
some barrels on the west side of the wharf. . . . He
stretched himself upon the plank and lay there until after
daybreak on the morning of the 6th. A gentleman passing by, noticed the man, and on seeing his face recognized
the poet. . . .

Where Moran had learned all this, why he hadn't come
forward with it earlier, are questions left unanswered. Predictably, because of the many obvious errors in the remainder of his text, not to mention overstatements and
distortions (even as to dates and such matters as how long
Poe had spent in the hospital), little serious attention was
paid to the Moran thesis. His little book was dismissed as
egregious grandstanding, a pitiful effort to cash in on the
accident of fate that had him on duty in the hospital that
critical afternoon.

In truth, no one could blame the dissenters for that
blunt opinion, especially when faced with the grandilo-
quent deathbed speeches Moran places in the mouth of the
nearly moribund Poe: "He who arched the Heavens and
upholds the Universe has His decrees legibly written upon
the frontlet of every human being," or "Death's dark angel
has done his work—language cannot express the terrific
tempest that sweeps over me," and so on. Moran even had
the chutzpah, if that is the word, to portray Poe, when re-
plying to a question about contacting his friends, actually
pronouncing as his answer the word, "Nevermore!"

Still, Moran *had,* of course, played a leading role in the tragedy. Also, for many years thereafter he'd been a resident of Baltimore, available to hear, and to be told, many things about Poe's last days—rumors and stories concerning the poet in that city during the last half of the century never abated. Moreover, Moran's booklet of 1885 was not his first retailing of the peculiar business of Poe, on his way to Philadelphia, suddenly stopping and coming back. In the *Herald* account of the dedication in 1875, he is quoted as saying much the same thing, in less detail and shorter compass.

Nor was Moran alone among the early commentators in his mention of that sudden return. In his 1877 volume, the initial attempt at Poe biography, William Gill had Poe in Baltimore stopping for a drink or two before boarding the Philadelphia train. "At Havre de Grace," wrote Gill, "the conductor of the train, finding him in a state of delirium, and knowing he had friends and relatives in Baltimore, brought him back to that city."

Aggravatingly, Gill too omits all mention of sources.

❦

Poe's luggage, what had become of *that,* it was asked, particularly the small traveling trunk. A sturdy, metal-bound case some two feet wide, the trunk had left Richmond with Poe. Yet, according to Neilson Poe, it had not been found during the search conducted in Baltimore immediately after Poe's death.

The little trunk and its whereabouts were among the first things that people thought of when trying to determine what had happened. The location of the trunk, it was thought, and perhaps its contents, should indicate *something* about Poe's movements and intentions in those last days. Here again, it was Dr. Moran who managed to play the leading role, succeeding where Neilson Poe had failed. At the end of October he tracked it down in storage at a hotel near the docks (Bradshaw's, he thought years later). Promptly he gave it to Neilson Poe, who shortly afterward sent it on to Mrs. Clemm, then living with Mrs. Annie Richmond in Lowell.

Disappointingly, the contents of the trunk revealed nothing about Poe's fate—there were some manuscripts, some books (Poe's own and others), some extra clothes and a few personal items. No one ever made a list of the trunk's contents, but judging by separate references, at least these things may be taken as certain.

More than the trunk's contents, it was the *place* in which it was found that bore significance. But no one then could have guessed it.

❧ 5 ❧

Five Lost Days

*iming.* From the start, that was the question occupying most minds, sequence and timing. If Poe was picked up in Baltimore on the afternoon of October 3rd, having departed Richmond early on the morning of September 27th, where had he been for those intervening five days, and with whom? Never had there been any reliable reports by people claiming to have met or seen him during that blank stretch. There were only one or two vague and unsupported rumors, put forward years later, obvious instances of biography abhorring a vacuum. None led anywhere.

For more than two full decades the puzzle of the five lost days continued to tantalize. Then in an article in *Harper's Magazine* for September 1872, a statement was made—bare of evidence but offered confidently—which seemed to account for at least several of them (also, curiously, an-

ticipating the peculiar Havre de Grace incident). Written
by R. H. Stoddard, the article was a brief, rather unsym-
pathetic sketch of Poe's life. Concerning his last hours, it
concludes:

> . . . the facts, as far as they can be ascertained, appear to
> be these: He arrived at Baltimore safely, but between
> trains unfortunately he took a drink with a friend, the
> consequence of which was that he was brought back from
> Havre de Grace by the conductor of the Philadelphia
> train, in a state of delirium. It was the eve of an exciting
> municipal election, and as he wandered up and down the
> streets of Baltimore he was seized by the lawless agents
> of some political club, and shut up all night in a cellar.
> The next morning he was taken out in a state of frenzy,
> drugged, and made to vote in eleven different wards. The
> following day he was found in a back room of a "head-
> quarters," and removed to a hospital.

A leading New York City editor-writer of the day, Stoddard nowhere states how and where he obtained his information. But the troubling lack of support for the unusual
claim prompted no dispute, nor did it prevent its acceptance, at least in some quarters. Within two years it appeared in print again, this time in an article in *The Southern
Magazine* for August 1874 (a Baltimore publication). A
lengthy treatment of Poe's life in general, it was written
by a Baltimore journalist, William Baird, who had connections with both the magazine and its editor, the respected
William Hand Browne.

Baird's claim about election violence is made in only a
few words—easily identified as a close paraphrase of the
Stoddard passage—again presented as if it were a mere

recital of established fact. The unwary Poe, wrote Baird, reaching Baltimore on his way north, became "the victim of the most brutal ill-treatment, which probably caused his death. It was the day before an exciting city election, and he is said to have been confined all night in a cellar, then drugged the next day, and carried around to be voted at eleven different wards. The day afterwards he was taken to a hospital in a state of insensibility."

As with Stoddard, it was a curiously bare statement for so radical an explanation, one coming to light so late in the game. Some slight added discussion of its implications, some measure of corroborating detail, would have been quite in order. But Baird, like his predecessor, missed his chance. At the same time behind the scenes, however, the editor of *The Southern Magazine* was busy supplying just such added information, in this case to a prospective Poe biographer, the competent, capable John Ingram (then researching what would prove to be the first generally reliable life of the poet).

Sending a copy of the Baird paper to Ingram, the editor took some pains in his letter to explain matters:

> At that time, and for years before and after, there was an infamous custom in this and other cities, at election time, of "cooping" voters. That is, gangs of men picked up, inveigled, or even carried off by force, men whom they found in the streets (generally the poor, friendless, or strangers) and transported them to cellars in various slums of the city, where they were kept under guard, threatened, maltreated if they attempted to escape, often robbed, and always compelled to drink whiskey (frequently drugged) until they were stupefied and helpless.

At the election these miserable wretches were brought up to the polls in carts or omnibuses, under guard, and made to vote the tickets in their hands. Death from the ill-treatment was not very uncommon. The general belief here is, that Poe was seized by one of these gangs (his death happening just at election-time; an election for sheriff took place on October 4th), "cooped," stupefied with liquor, dragged out and voted, then turned adrift to die. . . .

As some corroboration, Browne in his letter gives an extract from a volume published that same year, by the historian J. T. Scharf, *Chronicles of Baltimore.* Referring to the elections of 1858, Scharf wrote: "The Reform Association was organized to secure quiet and fairness at the polls, which at this time were scenes of the most disgraceful violence and disorder. In addition to the ordinary acts of riot and intimidation, honest gentlemen as well as unfortunate wretches were frequently seized and 'cooped' in vile dens, drugged, stupefied with whiskey, and then carried round and 'voted' in ward after ward, the police offering no opposition, and the judges receiving the votes." The custom, added Browne, had prevailed for many years, but at last the outrages "had grown so flagrant that law-abiding citizens associated to put down ruffianism, armed themselves, and extinguished it."

With all that, the question of evidence tying Poe to the "cooping," and of sources, was not addressed. Nor was it made clear who first thought of the vicious practice as possibly supplying the answer to the riddle of Poe's last days. The identity of the originator of that idea, perhaps, could not have been known to or discovered by many people at the time, certainly not among the general public. But now, with so much additional documentation on hand, it is possible to answer the question with complete confidence.

The formulator, or originator, of the theory that Poe was an unfortunate victim of election violence turns out to be his old friend and colleague in Richmond, John R. Thompson, editor of the *Messenger.* He first put the idea forth in a lecture, written by himself, "The Genius and Character of Edgar Allan Poe," delivered a number of times in cities north and south during the late sixties and up to his death in April 1873. One of the cities in which he spoke was Baltimore, where interest in Poe was high, especially regarding his death, and where he was an intimate of his fellow editor, William Hand Browne.

But during all that same five-year period Thompson was no longer resident in Richmond. In 1867 he left Virginia and went to New York City, where he served as literary editor for the prestigious *Evening Post* under William Cullen Bryant. While researching and preparing his lecture on Poe, in which he gives election violence as the cause of his death, Thompson was in frequent personal touch with another of the city's front-line editors, R. H. Stoddard (in the *Harper's* article, aside from the topic of election violence, there is ample indication to show that Stoddard did in fact use Thompson as a source).

John Thompson, it can be seen, in addition to being the originator of the idea, was also the one who, through Stoddard and the influential pages of *Harper's,* then the *Southern Magazine,* deliberately put it into print. In that fact resides a peculiar significance, unsuspected at the time and ever afterward.

Thompson's version of the "cooping," as it appears in the printed version of the old lecture (not published until 1929), is the blueprint for all that has since been said of it. There are some differences, and one large error (about Poe's reason for the trip), but mostly it is the same:

> The manner of his death was as painful as it was extraordinary. On his way through Baltimore to fulfill a literary engagement with a northern publisher he either, as some say, gave way to his besetting sin, or he was drugged. Adrift upon the streets of that large city, on the eve of an exciting municipal election, he was seized by the lawless agents of a political club, imprisoned in a cellar for the night, and taken out next day in a state bordering on frenzy and made to vote in eleven different wards, as if in half-pitiable, half-ludicrous compensation for never having exercised the right of suffrage before. Cast off at the close of the polls by his vulgar and brutal tyrants of a day, he was humanely taken by strangers to a hospital. . . .

The hope cherished by Ingram, that he might be the first formal biographer to give the cooping theory was defeated in 1877 when a competitor, William Gill, brought out his own volume. Drawing on the Baird article, Gill in very brief fashion states the supposed facts as if they were unquestioned: Poe had been seized by political roughs, locked overnight in a cell where he was drugged, then taken out next morning and "made to repeat votes at eleven different wards." (The "eleven" wards, of course, had reached Baird through Stoddard from Thompson, who never said how he knew, or could have known, the precise number.) Gill's book, however, was short and superficial, an anemic affair, and made little impact. Ingram still had his chance to score a significant first in Poe biography, and he took full advantage of it.

Using the material on Poe's death sent from Baltimore by Browne, Ingram proceeded to expand it with stray bits from a variety of other printed sources, none of them provable, but handy for life-giving detail. With the Ingram volume, published in 1880, the cooping theory of Poe's demise became more or less fixed in the literature. Often denied in whole or in part, sometimes abruptly dismissed ("twaddle," was all T. O. Mabbott deigned to say), it has never been quite laid aside. Poe, wrote Ingram, upon leaving Richmond for New York,

> proceeded by boat to Baltimore, which city he reached safely on the morning following his departure. Upon his arrival he gave his trunk to a porter to convey it, it is stated, to the cars which were timed to leave in an hour or so for Philadelphia, whilst he sought some refreshment. What now happened is still shrouded in mystery: before leaving Richmond the poet had complained of indisposition; of chilliness, and of exhaustion, and it is just possible that the increase of these symptoms may have enticed him into breaking his pledge, or into resorting to some deleterious drug.
>
> Be the cause whatever it may, it now appears to have become the fixed belief of the Baltimoreans, that the unfortunate poet, while in a state of temporary mania or stupor, fell into the hands of a gang of ruffians who were scouring the streets in search of victims. Wednesday the 3rd of October was election day for members of Congress in the state of Maryland, and it is the general supposition that Poe was captured by an electioneering band,

"cooped," drugged, dragged to the polls, and then, after having voted the ticket placed in his hand, was ruthlessly left in the street to die. For the truth of this terrible tale there appears too great a probability.

The porter conveying the trunk to the train depot, Poe indulging meanwhile in some "refreshment," are assertions that go unproved. That the election on October 3rd was not alone for local office but for the United States Congress was true, a fact Ingram was first to record. Yet, while giving the cooping theory at its fullest, he neatly avoids taking responsibility for it—in Baltimore it was a "fixed belief." Then he closes with a rather deft mention of "probability."

To this point the cooping theory had progressed without the benefit of any real evidence linking the poet to the practice. The fact that he had been found near a polling place on election day had been mentioned rather promptly, in the *Herald* story, to start. Neilson Poe in a letter, and Snodgrass in print had both referred to it. But few were conscious of the circumstance as something significant until Baird and Browne, in 1874, began to emphasize it. Then in 1880, with discovery of the original Walker note, the two felt sure that the theory had been clinched.

In some excitement, Browne fired off the good news to Ingram, adding it to a letter already half-finished. "Since writing the other leaf," he exclaims, "a new and very important Poe-annal has turned up among Dr. Snodgrass's papers. It is the letter from the election-coop asking Snodgrass to come to Poe's help—thus putting the 'cooping' incident beyond a doubt. I have copied it from the original, and this is the text," upon which he inserts the full note precisely.

Of course, Browne in his delight at the find was according the Walker note far too much weight as evidence. All it really did on the cooping question was corroborate the earlier, desultory references to the *site*. Browne's assumption that Ryan's Tavern was itself the "election-coop" must soon have been seen as wildly inaccurate: a motley crowd of drugged and liquored men huddled in Ryan's cellar would hardly have been overlooked by the election judges monitoring the flow of voters upstairs (three judges were assigned to each poll, according to the day's papers). There was also the police "watch," on increased patrol during any election.

The culminating stroke in the cooping theory, assuring its survival in some form in Poe biography, came with an article published in March 1881, again in the New York *Herald*. In close collaboration with editor Browne, a reporter on the Baltimore *Sun* named Edward Spencer had researched the story, hoping especially to find that Joseph Walker was still alive. Rather promptly it was found that Walker had died years before, a victim of an accidental drowning, disappointingly leaving no additional information to be passed on about his fateful encounter. All Spencer learned of Walker was that he'd served at some time in the *Sun*'s printing plant, as well as having worked for Snodgrass as a typesetter. The wording of his note to Snodgrass seemed to deny the possibility, inferred by many afterward, that he knew Poe and had recognized him at Ryan's. In that case, why he had stopped to talk with the inebriated man became a tantalizing question.

Undaunted, Spencer then began digging deeper, looking into the supposed coop itself, even hoping to turn up some of its old occupants. As Browne wrote, Spencer was "hunt-

ing up all about Ryan's place, & will try to see if any of
Poe's fellow-prisoners in that den can now be found . . . [he]
will then prepare a paper for one of the magazines." The
paper that appeared, five months later, was a long one, dealing with other Poe items in addition to the Walker note.
What it had to say of Walker, however, and the cooping
business, was easily the most compelling part.

Pointing out that Ryan's place, in Lombard Street, was
only a door or two away from the corner of High Street,
he adds that Snodgrass lived on High Street, hardly two
blocks from the tavern. Probably, he suggests, it was this
"immediate proximity as much as anything else which
prompted Walker to send for him," rather than for someone
else. It was a good guess, though it assumes that Walker
knew where Snodgrass lived, and it slights the fact that
Poe, when questioned by Walker, managed to pronounce
Snodgrass' name.

What really engaged Spencer's attention, and of course
that of Browne as well, was the description of Poe that
Snodgrass gave in his *Beadle's* article of fourteen years before. Quoting from the Walker note, Spencer indignantly
rejects the Snodgrass phrase—"in a state of beastly intoxication and evident destitution"—contrasting it with
Walker's milder reference to "a gentleman rather the worse
for wear," who was in need of assistance. Walker, concluded Spencer, had pictured only "a man so ill as to excite"
the sympathy of a passerby. Yet Snodgrass saw him as "a
drunken and penniless loafer."

With that, Spencer let loose a barrage of fact-mixed-with-
guesses calculated to leave no doubt as to the full reality of
the cooping idea, and its responsibility for Poe's death. He
begins by permitting himself one small assumption, that

Poe in Baltimore, while waiting to catch the evening train to Philadelphia, would have stopped for a rest at the United States Hotel, just opposite the railway depot:

> Eight blocks east of the hotel was High Street, and in the rear of an engine-house in this vicinity the "Fourth Ward Club," a notorious whig organization, had their "coop." There was no registry of voters at this time in Baltimore, and almost anyone could vote who was willing to face the ordeal of a "challenge," and the oath administered by the judge of elections. . . .
>
> The roughs of the period, instead of acting as rounders themselves, used to capture and "coop" innocent strangers and foreigners, drug them with bad whiskey and opiates, and send them round to different voting-places under custody of one or two of their party. . . .
>
> If the writer's memory does not play him a trick, the coop of the Democrats on Lexington Street, near Eutaw, in the rear of the "New Market engine-house," had 75 prisoners, while that of the Whigs, on High Street, had 130 to 140. . . .
>
> The prisoners in these "coops," chiefly foreigners, strangers, and countrymen, fared wretchedly. They were often, at the outstart and in the most unexpected way, drugged with opiates and such other delirifacients as would be most likely to keep them from being troublesome. . . .
>
> They were thrust into cellars and backyards, and kept under lock and key, without lights, without beds, without provisions for decency, without food. Only one thing they were supplied with, and that was a sufficient deluge of whiskey to keep their brains all the time sodden. . . .
>
> The Whig coop in the Fourth Ward on High Street was within two squares of the place where Poe was

"found." It is altogether possible that Poe was cooped, and his outlaw custodians, discovering too late the disastrous effects of their infamous decoctions upon the delicate tissues and convolutions of his finely organized brain, sought to repair some of the damage they had done, and caused inquiry to be made for the friends of the man they had murdered. Too late!

How the sympathetic Walker was meant to fit into that final surprising charge is none too clear. Spencer's phrasing at this point, of course, may be inept. Yet he does seem to place Walker among the "outlaw custodians," makes him at least aware of what had transpired behind the scenes. But the suggestion itself—having hardboiled political lackeys caring what happened to one out of the hundreds of men they debauched—is strained.

After Spencer and Ingram, for three quarters of a century the cooping story kept its place in Poe biography. For some it was a strong possibility, for others nearly certain, especially those anxious to have the onus for what happened removed from Poe to a third party. Then it simply began to fade away, not contradicted by clear evidence or by argument to the contrary, but as the victim of scholarly ennui. For too long it had been in play without acquiring real support or enlivening detail, nothing even to create controversy. Its last full-fledged appearance was in the respected 1941 biography by A. H. Quinn. Thereafter it dwindled away until in the most recent reference volume of importance on Poe studies it is dismissed in one word, "fanciful." In the latest full-scale scholarly biography, that by Kenneth Silverman in 1991, it gets no mention at all. Jumping from the day of Poe's Richmond departure on September 27th to the afternoon he was found, the Silverman narrative leaves only a blank between.

Curiously, in all the research expended on this idea, one relevant question has been consistently ignored (dodged, it almost seems): what had the Baltimore newspapers to report about the day's activities? With so much rough "cooping" going on all over the city—apparently hundreds of poor souls being rounded up and maltreated—did any reporters spot these criminal infractions? Were there no complaints to the police? The Baltimore *Sun* of October 4th said that all day on the 3rd rain had fallen off and on, keeping the voter turnout small:

> There was very little excitement in the city during the day, and not much more at night. The election passed off quite harmoniously, and we heard of no disturbances at the polls or elsewhere. The voting progressed steadily, exhibiting only the impulses incident to the variations of the weather, and the occasional appearance of voters by the dozen or score. As the returns began to come in, the successful party became a little musical, and throughout the early part of the evening bonfires illuminated the streets, and discharges of gunpowder in various forms celebrated the victory.

But if there is no real support, no actual evidence, hard or soft, for the "cooping" theory, then how and why was it ever conceived? What was it that moved John R. Thompson to put forth such an offbeat claim? For that question there *is* an answer. But it must await its turn to be told.

❦

The night that Elmira watched the slight, black-clad figure of the departing Poe descend the front steps of her home and walk off into the darkness was the last on which anyone definitely saw him alive, or so it was believed for many years. Only after the turn of the century did reliable information surface placing him elsewhere in Richmond that night.

Upon leaving Elmira he stopped in at the office of Dr. John Carter, a ten-minute walk from the Shelton residence. This is not conjecture, derived at second hand, for the revelation was made by Dr. Carter himself in his old age. Acquainted for years with the MacKenzie family, Carter had met Poe socially any number of times during his stay in the city. As the reason for Poe's visit to him that night, he says only that the office provided him with a "resting place" when walking back from Elmira's house into town. He doesn't say why a doctor's office would have been open so late.

At Carter's, Poe lingered for a while talking with the doctor—nothing is said of medical attention—then he remarked that he would stroll across to a local restaurant on Main Street, Sadler's, some three blocks away. Leaving the office he somehow took, not his own walking stick, but that of the doctor, a distinctive Malacca specimen that concealed a sword in its slim, brown, innocent-looking length. In the South of that day every man with pretensions to gentility sported a cane. During his stay in Richmond in 1849, it is known, Poe had readily adopted the practice.

The Carter revelations appeared in an article in *Lippincott's Magazine* for November 1902, teasingly entitled, "Edgar Poe's Last Night in Richmond." Since it is an important document in the case, and has never been reprinted before, it deserves a fuller place in this record than paraphrase. Most of it treats, not that crucial night but various aspects of Poe's life, and only in the closing paragraphs are the relevant hours covered.

Carter, then a young beginning doctor, aged twenty-four, had become friendly with Poe that final summer in Richmond, meeting him at Duncan Lodge, the MacKenzie home, and other places. Neglecting to mention dates, he says he hadn't seen Poe for some days, when unexpectedly,

> one evening about half-past nine o'clock he called at my office, which, being on Seventeenth and Broad Streets afforded him a half-way resting place between Duncan Lodge and the residence of Mrs. Shelton. . . . He sat for some time talking, while playing with a handsome Malacca sword-cane recently presented me by a friend, and then abruptly rising, said, "I think I will step over to Saddler's (a popular restaurant of the neighborhood) for a few minutes," and so left without any further word, having my cane still in his hand.
>
> From this manner of departure I inferred that he expected to return shortly, but did not see him again, and was surprised to learn next day that he had left for Baltimore by the early morning boat. I then called on Saddler, who informed me that Poe had left his house [restaurant?] at exactly twelve that night, starting for the Baltimore boat in company with several companions whom he had met at Saddler's, and giving as a reason therefor the lateness of the hour and the fact that the boat was to leave at four o'clock.
>
> According to Saddler he was in good spirits and sober, though it is certain that he had been drinking and that he seemed oblivious of his baggage, which had been left in his room at the Swan Tavern.

Carter's action next day in inquiring after Poe was fortunate, for it produced the only contemporary firsthand assertion that Poe did actually leave town that morning, and by steamer rather than by rail. His source for the information, Sadler, the restaurant proprietor, deserves more credence, certainly, than would some vaguer, less closely linked party—it seems that Poe, as a regular customer, was known to Sadler on a personal basis. Just who those "several companions" were who joined Poe as he ate, and then at or about midnight were kind enough to escort him aboard the Baltimore steamer is nowhere stated, nowhere even guessed at.

That was all. For nearly a hundred years, now, nothing more of significance has come to light. The mystery of Poe's death, in the face of endless probing, is back where it began on that dismal afternoon of October 3rd, 1849, when the kindly Joseph Walker entered Ryan's bar and stopped to talk to a gentleman obviously in need of assistance.

{ 6 }

The Sartain Interval

o real difficulty exists as to where, with what single solid piece of evidence, the investigation of Poe's untimely death should begin. Fairly leaping out of the jumble of information surrounding that sad event is the matter of his nondescript apparel when found, at least some of it not his own.

The strange clothing, in fact, was one aspect of the barroom scene which struck Snodgrass so forcibly that he twice reported it in some detail. Since a shabby appearance is totally at odds with all that is known of Poe's sartorial habits, it is fair to say that the fact itself demands attention somewhat urgently.

With that decision, a door immediately swings open, for in the record of that last summer of Poe's life can be found two other references to the matter of his personal appearance, both of them quite arresting in their implications. They are referred, however, not to his last hours in October, but to the days of early July, just before he reached Richmond on his way south. Curiously, one of them depicts his own deliberate effort to change his appearance, in fact to disguise himself.

Both incidents occurred during his stopover in Philadelphia where, it is well known, he fell into one of his periodic drinking sprees. Both involve his being aided by friends, with the facts put on record by the friends themselves. How the two accounts might fit together is the first question to be answered, in particular with regard to the evident emphasis on Poe's appearance.

First of the two to go on record was George Lippard, another impecunious author, aged twenty-seven, and an old acquaintance of Poe's. Just four years after Poe's death, Lippard set down, somewhat briefly, his memory of an unexpected visit he had received from Poe in his office in Philadelphia "on a hot summer day," not otherwise dated. The visitor was, recalled Lippard, in a state of severe despondency, "poorly clad and with but one shoe on his feet. . . . He came stealthily upstairs, as if conscious that he was an intruder anywhere."

Seating himself dejectedly at a table, Poe blurted to the shocked Lippard that "he had no bread to eat—no place to sleep—not one friend in God's world." This was Lippard's first sight of Poe in some time, in fact since Poe's own Philadelphia residence five years before. Painfully recalling happier days, Lippard felt instant sympathy for the downcast poet, so "shabbily clad," as he said, who was now asking for a loan to pay his way to Richmond. Himself struggling with financial woes, Lippard had not a penny to spare, so when Poe suggested that he might apply on his behalf to various editors and publishers, he readily agreed.

"Tell them that I am sick," he quotes Poe as calling after him as he went out. "That I haven't a bed to sleep upon. That I only want enough to get me out of Philadelphia. . . . For God's sake don't fail me! You're my last hope!"

While Poe waited in Lippard's office, his friend went round to several men whom he knew were well acquainted with Poe, either personally or through his writings. Five of them made contributions. Next day a somewhat recovered Poe, calmer and full of gratitude, was accompanied to the train by Lippard and one or two others not named. They put him aboard and "never saw him again."

The two terms, "poor" and "shabby," applied by Lippard to Poe's attire that day leave open the question of what, exactly, was meant. Were the words intended to describe good clothes that were in disrepair and soiled? Or did they indicate a cheap sort of coat and trousers, rougher common apparel below the standards of a gentleman—much more conspicuous a matter then than now? The article gives no clue, and about all that may be remarked, in a tentative way, concerns Lippard's generous journey round town soliciting funds. The questions are obvious:

Why couldn't Poe have managed this unpleasant chore for himself, instead of imposing it on someone he hadn't seen or been in touch with for a very long while? Why was it necessary for Poe to remain in the office, waiting? Was he kept there by his shabby appearance, or by something else? Surely another shoe could have been found to take the place of the missing one, if that is what prevented him from going abroad in the city. This is really a very pertinent question, and a legitimate one, inescapable on a close reading of the Lippard account, describing an event then no more than four years in the past.

At that time, Lippard himself, as he clearly states, was feeling very sick (cholera had hit the city, as it had many other places along the eastern seaboard in the middle months of 1849). While making his rounds, in fact, Lippard became even sicker, and had "just enough strength" to get back home. Next morning after daybreak he was better and went down to his office with the money. "I thought you had deserted me!" breathed a grateful Poe.

There, for the moment, the unhappy Lippard interlude may be allowed to rest, while the second Philadelphia tableau—so to call it—so much resembling the first, is reviewed.

Centering on the publisher John Sartain, the second incident is much better known than the other, and is also of much greater complication, amounting at places to actual confusion. But the complication can be unraveled, the confusion shown to have a quite definite and reasonable basis, giving rise to one crucial fact never yet suspected. To get at that fact, to show how it is derived, it is necessary to view the original statement nearly at its fullest. However, this is not a simple matter, since Sartain told the story several times, at more or less length, during a period of twenty-five years.

In the fall of 1849, Sartain was forty-one years old. Poe he had known for a decade, not socially but professionally, the two having first met when working together on *Graham's Magazine* in Philadelphia (Sartain as an engraver, Poe as sub-editor). Later their careers diverged but they remained on friendly terms, Sartain especially showing great respect and admiration for Poe's varied talents. By 1849, Sartain had become proprietor of the influential *Union Magazine,* and was a power in the world of American letters. Longfellow, Thoreau, Lowell, Simms, Martineau, were a few of the well-known names that had appeared in the *Union*'s glossy pages.

Sartain first went on record with his memories of Poe in 1875, when he gave the story in detail to biographer William Gill. Next was an article in *Lippincott's Magazine* for March 1889. Then came an interview in the Philadelphia *Press* for June 1892, followed the next year by a lengthy, first-person statement in the Philadelphia *Record* (reprinted in the Boston *Transcript* and other papers). Lastly, there was a ten-page section in Sartain's autobiography of 1899, which proves to be almost a verbatim copy of the *Lippincott's* piece.

To gain a comprehensive picture of the incident in question, it is necessary to take a glance—with some more than a glance—at all five sources, starting with a fairly sustained look at the fullest of the presentations, the one in *Lippincott's*. After opening with a discussion of Poe's poem, *The Bells,* published earlier in his own magazine, Sartain goes on at some length, and an attentive reader will detect clear signs of the confusion mentioned above, at places even outright contradiction:

> The last time I saw Mr. Poe was in 1849, and then under such peculiar and fearful conditions that it can never fade from my memory. Early one Monday afternoon he suddenly made his appearance in my engraving-room, looking pale and haggard and with a wild expression in his eyes. I did not let him see that I had noticed it, and, shak-

ing his hand warmly, invited him to be seated, when he began: "Mr. Sartain, I have come to you for protection and a refuge. It will be difficult for you to believe what I have to tell—that such things could be in this nineteenth century. It is necessary that I remain concealed for a time. Can I stay here with you?"

"Certainly," said I, "as long as you like: you will be perfectly safe here." He thanked me and then went into an explanation of what was the matter.

He said that he was on his way to New York, when he overheard some men who sat a few seats back of him plotting how they would kill him and throw him from the platform of the car. He said they spoke so low it would have been impossible for him to hear and understand the meaning of their words, had it not been that his sense of hearing was so acute. They did not guess that he had heard them, as he sat so quiet and suppressed all indication of having heard the plot.

He watched an opportunity to give them the slip at Bordentown, and when the train arrived at that station he stepped to the platform and kept out of sight till the train had moved on again. He had returned to Philadelphia by the first return conveyance, and had hurried to me for shelter.

I assured him that he was perfectly welcome, but that it was my belief that the whole thing was the creation of his fancy, for what interest could these people have in taking his life, and at such risk to themselves?

He said, "It was for revenge."

"Revenge for what?" said I.

He answered, "Well, a woman trouble."

I placed him comfortably, and then went on with my work, which was in a hurry. Occasionally conversation passed between us, and I observed a singular change in the current of his thoughts. He had rushed in on me in terror for his life, in fear that he might be killed, and now I perceived that he had drifted round to the idea that it would be good to kill himself.

After a long silence he said suddenly, "If this moustache of mine were removed I should not be so readily recognized. Will you lend me a razor, that I may shave it off?" I told him that, as I never shaved, I had no razor, but if he wanted it removed I could do that for him almost as close with a scissors. Accordingly, I took him to the bathroom and performed the operation successfully.

After tea, it being now dark, he prepared to go out, and on my asking him where he was going, he said, "To the Schuylkill." I told him I would go too, to which he offered no objection. His shoes were worn down a good deal on the outer side of the heels, and he complained that his feet were chafed in consequence, and hurt him, so I gave him my slippers to wear, as I had no second pair of shoes that would serve. When we had reached the corner of Ninth and Chestnut Streets we waited there for an omnibus, and among the things he said was that he wished I would see to it that after his death the painting Osgood had made of him should go to his mother (meaning Mrs. Clemm). I promised him that as far as I could control it, that should be done.

We entered an omnibus and rode to its stopping-place, a tavern on the north side of Callowhill Street, on the bend it takes toward the northwest to reach the Fairmount Bridge. At this place there was light enough, chiefly from what shone out through the door of the tavern, but beyond was darkness, and forward into the darkness we went.

I kept on his left side, and on nearly approaching the bridge I guided him off to the right by a gentle pressure until we reached the foot of the lofty flight of steep

wooden steps that ascended almost to the top of the res-
ervoir. Here was the first landing, and with seats, so we
sat down. All this time I had contrived to keep him in
conversation, which never ceased except when we were on
our way up that breakneck flight of stairs. I had reckoned
on the moon's rising, but it did not: I had forgotten that
each evening it rose so much later. There we sat at that
dizzy height in perfect darkness, for clouds hid the stars,
and I hoping for the moon which came not.

As they sat, Poe went on talking, now telling of a random series of "visions," or hallucinations he'd had while
being held in Moyamensing Prison. One was of a radiant
female figure who directed a stream of questions at him,
his fate depending on his answers. Another was a caldron
of boiling liquid, presented to him with the threat that
he would be "lifted by the hair or my head and dipped
into the hot liquid up to my lips, like Tantalus." Last was a
horrific scene showing, to Poe's tortured horror, Mrs. Clemm
being dismembered. Sartain goes on:

These are examples of the kind of talk I listened to up
there in the darkness; but, as everything has an end, so
had this, and we descended the steep stairway slowly and
cautiously, holding well on to the handrails. By still keeping him talking I got him back to an omnibus that waited
for passengers at the tavern door, and when exactly abreast
of the step I pressed against him and raised his foot to it,
but instantly recollecting himself, he drew back, when I
gently pushed him, saying "Go on," and having got him
seated with myself beside him, said, "You were saying so
and so," and he responded by continuing the subject he
had been speaking on.
I took him safe home to Sansom Street, gave him a bed

on the sofa in the dining-room, and slept alongside of him on three chairs, without undressing.

On the second morning he seemed to have become so much like his old self that I trusted him to go out alone. Regular meals and a rest had a good effect; but his mind was not yet free from all nightmare. After an hour or two he returned, then he told me that he had arrived at the conclusion that what I said was true, that the whole thing had been a delusion and a scare created out of his own excited imagination. He said that his mind began to clear as he lay on the grass, his face buried in it, and his nostrils inhaling its sweet fragrance mingled with the odor of the earth; that the words he had heard kept running through his mind, but somehow he tried in vain to connect them with who spoke them, and thus his thoughts gradually awakened into rational order and he saw that he came out of a dream.

I had asked him how he came to be in Moyamensing Prison, and he said he had been suspected of trying to pass a fifty-dollar counterfeit note; but the truth is it was for what takes so many there for a few hours only, the drop too much. . . . Being now all right again, he was ready to go to New York. He borrowed what was needful, and departed. I never saw him more.

Quite plainly evident is the fact that two different situations are involved here, but have been described as if they are one, the author apparently unaware of his error. But detailed comment may be postponed in order to compare a shorter version of the same incident, the one that appeared in the Philadelphia *Record* (as reprinted in the Boston *Transcript*). Here again, that same contradiction is present, again with the writer seemingly unaware that he is treating as one what are really two different situations:

The first instance of hallucination I ever detected in Poe occurred about a month before his tragic death. I was at work in my shirt-sleeves, in my office on Sansom Street, when Poe burst in upon me excitedly, and exclaimed, "I have come to you for refuge." I saw at a glance that he was suffering from some mental overstrain, and assured him of shelter. I then begged him to explain.

"I was just on my way to New York on the train," he said to me, "when I heard whispering going on behind me. Owing to my marvelous power of hearing I was enabled to overhear what the conspirators were saying. Just imagine such a thing in this nineteenth century! They were plotting to murder me. I immediately left the train and hastened back here again. I must disguise myself in some way. I must shave off this moustache at once. Will you lend me a razor?"

Afraid to trust him with it, I told him I hadn't any, but that I could remove his moustache with the scissors. Taking him to the rear of the office I sheared away until he was absolutely barefaced. This satisfied him somewhat and I managed to calm him.

That very evening, however, he prepared to leave the house. "Where are you going?" I asked. "To the Schuylkill," he replied. "Then I am going along with you," I declared. He did not object, and together we walked to Chestnut Street and took a bus.

A steep flight of steps used to lead up from the Schuylkill then, and ascending these we sat on a bench overlooking the stream. The night was black, without a star, and I felt somewhat nervous alone with Poe in the condition he was in. Going up in the bus he said to me, "after my death see that my mother (Mrs. Clemm) gets that portrait of me from Osgood."

Now he began to talk the wildest nonsense, in the weird, dramatic style of his tales. He said he had been thrown into Moyamensing Prison for forging a check, and while there a white female form had appeared on the battlements and addressed him in whispers. . . .

Here again are recounted Poe's hallucinations, the supposed "visions," of the female figure and the caldron of boiling liquid (the scene with Mrs. Clemm is not given). The details are sparser but exactly the same as before. The conclusion of the account is also the same as the earlier version, but again not so developed:

> By and by I suggested we descend again and Poe assented. All the way down the steep steps I trembled lest he should remember his resolve of suicide, but I kept his mind from it and got him back safely. Three days after, he went out again and returned in the same mood. "I lay on the earth with my nose in the grass," he said then, "and the smell revived me. I began at once to realize the falsity of my hallucinations."

If it is not apparent at first, then a very few minutes of close attention to Sartain's two texts soon uncovers the curious fact that he shows Poe simultaneously in the grip of two different moods, both powerful, both directly opposite, contradictory. In one mood the poet arrives in Sartain's office mortally afraid of being murdered, frantically seeking a place to hide, and eager to disguise himself. In the other mood he is found, suddenly and with no good reason given, bent on suicide—"drifted round to the idea that it would be good to kill himself," according to the *Lippincott's* text. In the *Transcript* there is no drifting round to suicide, it is just *there,* abruptly replacing the fear of being murdered that was expressed a few paragraphs earlier. "All the way down the steep steps," explains Sartain as if he'd been talking of suicide all along, "I trembled lest he should remember his resolve of suicide."

Abject fear of murder by shadowy assassins, on the one hand, and a grim purpose of self-destruction, on the other—the two states of mind simply do not fit together. Writing forty and more years after the fact, Sartain has here unconsciously blended, ellided, woven clumsily together, two separate incidents of which he had personal knowledge. In a preliminary way, the obvious conclusion is that the two incidents occurred fairly close in time, and were similar in character, so that the blurring and the melding had a deceptively rational feel.

In one incident, Poe rushes in on Sartain begging for shelter ("burst in"), saying that he is in dire peril, that there are people trying to kill him. In the other, he shows himself so obviously suicidal that Sartain is sorely afraid that the poet may hurl himself to death from a height—perhaps taking Sartain with him, he adds in his autobiography, the two plunging "into the black depths below."

An added sign that the two incidents were originally separate is found in the story as it was supplied to Gill in 1875, its earliest form. In the Gill volume there is no mention at all of suicide. Everything is referred to Poe's "dread of some fearful conspiracy against his life." Sartain, continues Gill, was unable to "convince him that some deadly foe was not, at that very moment, in pursuit of him. He begged for a razor for the purpose of removing the moustache from his lip in order, as he suggested, that he might disguise his appearance and thus baffle his pursuers." When the story was first told, it can be seen, the idea of suicide was wholly absent.

At this point the question becomes, when did each of the two incidents take place, and under what circumstances? Somewhat surprisingly, what may seem a thorny problem, having no clear point of departure, actually proves to be rather plain, a matter simple in the extreme. The necessary clue is found in one of Poe's own letters, written from Philadelphia on July 7th to Mrs. Clemm. Starkly, it shows him sunk in a suicidal frame of mind, brought on by remorse over having again fallen victim to the bottle.

"The very instant you get this come to me," he raves in abject self-disgust. "The joy of seeing you will almost compensate for our sorrows. We can but die together. It's no use to reason with me *now;* I must die. I have no desire to live since I have done 'Eureka' . . . For your sake it would be sweet to live, but we must die together . . ." His inclusion of his devoted mother-in-law in the death-pact shows how much out of touch with reality he was at that moment, how far gone in blind self-loathing.

Mrs. Clemm did not come (the letter didn't reach her in New York until the crisis had passed), and in a few days Poe's crushing sense of degradation—as was usual with him in these cases—had dissipated. The letter he wrote Mrs. Clemm from his room in the American Hotel a week later, on July 14th, amply signals his recovery. He is still in anguish, still remorseful. All desire for the escape of death, however, has vanished.

The suicide thread in Sartain's mingled reminiscences, then, may be safely tied to Poe's two-week stopover in Philadelphia, July 1st to 13th. But having determined that much, the date of the other incident—the fear-of-murder thread—is also fixed. It occurred sometime in the five-day period between Poe's leaving Richmond on September 27th and his being found in Baltimore on October 3rd. Quite simply, there is no other time, not in 1849, not earlier, into which the interval can be fitted.

In other words, Poe in traveling north from Richmond that September did *not* halt his progress in Baltimore, remaining there until he was found, as has been generally accepted. From Baltimore he went on by train to Philadelphia, where some unexplained circumstance convinced him that he was the target of a murder plot. How long he stayed in Philadelphia, what happened while he was there, why he backtracked to Baltimore instead of going on to New York as planned—these are the questions now demanding an answer.

But in taking up that thread a final observation is in order regarding the claim that Poe did indeed get to Philadelphia during his last, fatal journey. It concerns the story told by conductor Rollins.

He had noticed Poe on his train headed for Philadelphia, said Rollins, and very soon afterward saw him on another train heading south for Baltimore again. As Rollins supposed, he had halted and changed trains at Havre de Grace on the Susquehanna. About that sudden halt, it is apparent, Rollins was speculating, indulging his imagination as he tried to account for the quick return. The valuable part of his testimony, the part that does not rely on interpretation, relates to the fundamental fact he states so assuredly: he saw Poe on a train bound north out of Baltimore, scheduled for a stop in Philadelphia.

❦

Sartain, at work in his office in Philadelphia, must have been more than a bit startled when Poe, "looking pale and haggard and with a wild expression in his eyes," burst in on him. He would have felt even more surprised to hear the story blurted by the excited poet. On the train speeding north to New York, explained Poe, he'd overheard some men who sat a few seats back of him "plotting how they would kill him" and throw him from the train. He'd been careful not to let on that he'd heard them, and had awaited his chance to "give them the slip at Bordentown." Boarding the next train back, he had returned to Philadelphia and hurried to his old colleague for shelter.

Taken aback, Sartain had managed to ask his visitor the obvious question—why would anyone want to kill him? "Revenge," was the stark answer, revenge for what Poe readily admitted was "woman trouble," letting it go at that. Even had he the temerity to ask, Sartain's curiosity as to who the woman was, and what Poe had done to deserve murdering, would have gone unsatisfied. No gentleman, in that day at least, on hearing the suggestive phrase, "woman trouble," would have presumed to inquire further.

The anxious Poe's most immediate concern, according to Sartain, was the task of altering his appearance to make himself less recognizable. For that purpose, of course, removal of the moustache made sense as a first step. When no razor was to be had in the office (Sartain at the time wore a beard), Poe readily submitted to having the job done for him with a scissors. If Sartain didn't simply forget—that he did overlook some details of the incident is of course quite likely— Poe did nothing else while with him to finish his disguise, or to clarify the situation. In fact, all the other details in Sartain's jumbled reminiscences—all of them—can be shown to refer to Poe's earlier visit, in July, when he had suicide on his mind. Everything else recorded by Sartain involves Poe going freely out into the city, riding busses, and strolling in full view, with the publisher or without him. But Poe's later visit, in September–October, was made in a frantic search "for shelter" from his mysterious pursuers, for "refuge." In that situation he would scarcely have ventured out, accompanied or not.

Analysis of the dates involved leads to no certainty as to chronology. Yet Poe's stay at the Sartain place could hardly have exceeded a night or two. In the several accounts of the incident, no special emphasis is placed on the matter of when or how Poe departed. In *Lippincott's,* Sartain concludes simply, "Being now all right again, he was ready to go to New York. He borrowed what was needful and departed. I never saw him more." His comment in the *Press* is similar: "Poe's mind became clearer in a day or two, and he left Philadelphia, after borrowing money for his expenses." True, those words can apply to either visit. But the reference to New York tips the probability in favor of September–October. In July, Poe had been headed south, to Richmond.

Leaving Sartain's place, his upper lip now naked, where did Poe head? The answer, again, is connected with the matter of his nondescript clothing when picked up drunk in Baltimore, some of the articles apparently not his own. No special flash of insight is needed to link *that* undoubted fact with the surprise felt by another Philadelphian on first seeing Poe's strangely drab and ungentlemanly appearance. George Lippard, greeting the downcast Poe as he "stealthily" entered his office, saw before him "a slender man poorly clad," described a few lines further along as "shabbily clad." *

---

* More than one sharp-eyed reader, I expect, will hasten to challenge my assertion that the Lippard incident, at least in part, refers to September–October rather than July. I suggest that, before firing, they consult the Notes.

In the hours between leaving Sartain's place and calling
in at Lippard's office, Poe had taken the time to complete
his "disguise," evidently stopping in at one or more of the
city's many secondhand clothing stores. Nervously greeting
the nonplussed Lippard, it may legitimately be said, Poe
was already dressed in the very same outlandish get-up he
would be wearing later when found by Snodgrass at Ryan's
Tavern: battered old palm-leaf hat, cheap alpaca coat, a
shirt of dingy white without either vest or necktie, baggy
trousers of commonplace material, dirty workman's boots.

But the testimony of the scissored moustache must not
be slighted. In its own way, that mundane little episode
provides surprisingly strong evidence for bolstering the
contention that Sartain's memory blindly intermingled two
separate situations, two months apart.

After Poe's arrival in Richmond on July 14th, a daguerreotype of him was taken in which his full moustache
is clearly and darkly visible. The date of the picture, made
at Pratt's Daguerrean Gallery on Main Street, is uncertain.
Usually it is given as September, even late September. But
the evidence for that dating is very soft (a guess by the
photographer, recorded long afterward) and the picture
may have been made much earlier. It could as easily have
been made within a week or so of his arrival, raising a problem of time.

Susan Talley, who was much struck by the poet's physical
presence, implies that when she first met Poe in Richmond
his upper lip was fully adorned. "He wore a dark moustache," she noted, "scrupulously kept." Their initial meeting she loosely records as happening "a day or two after"
he reached town. Of course, even if they met a week or
more after his arrival, there wouldn't have been enough

time for the re-growing. But if the scissoring was done, not in July, but on September 29–30, a matter of days before Poe was found in Baltimore, the supposed problem entirely disappears.

Unfortunately, of the few people who glimpsed Poe's face in those final days in Baltimore, at the tavern or the hospital, none remarked on the presence or absence of a moustache. Of course, those who saw him then and who had known him previously, hadn't encountered him for years. This includes Snodgrass, who took such careful note of his friend's poor, stricken face without saying whether the upper lip was bare.

{ 7 }

What Mrs. Smith Knew

n a small town in South Carolina, a few miles south of Charleston, forty-four years after the death of Poe, there died another American author, a woman well known at the time. Passing away in her extreme old age, she took with her what may have been the final necessary clue for the full and undoubted solution to the mystery of Poe's death. What she *did* leave on the record is just enough to tantalize and, in some satisfying degree, help point the way to the stark truth.

The attractive, accomplished Mrs. Elizabeth Oakes Smith first made Poe's acquaintance in New York City in 1845. A year or two before that, she and her husband with their four sons had come down from Portland, Maine, eager to take a leading role in the city's literary life. Both had already gained high reputations as prolific authors, in prose and poetry, and every month almost without fail saw their contributions gracing one or another of the leading journals. Her husband, Seba Smith, by then enjoyed a rather special niche as a popular author, riding on the success of his original character, Major Jack Downing, probably the first of America's comic sages and homespun commentators. In time, his wife's fame would surpass his own when she began writing novels and plays, and took up lecturing, one of the first women to mount the platform.

Many times in the years 1845–49 in New York, Mrs. Smith's path crossed that of Poe, the two meeting casually at the homes of mutual friends or at the city's frequent literary soirees, a custom then in full swing. At their initial encounter some strain may have been present, since Poe had previously said some harsh things in print about the poetry of both, the wife faring somewhat better than the husband. Regarding Mrs. Smith's most popular composition, a long poem of no less than sixteen hundred lines arranged in two hundred stanzas, titled *The Sinless Child,* while finding it full of flaws, Poe had actually conceded it great merit. "She has very narrowly missed one of those happy 'creations' which now and then immortalize the poet," he wrote, adding that with more thought and effort she might have made her poem "one of the best, if not the very best of American poems." It was the sort of exasperating comment at which Poe the critic was an adept, leaving its target hovering between gladness and resentment.

The rough treatment Poe had previously handed her husband's own long poem, *Powhatan,* published in 1841, would have been harder to forgive. In the influential pages of *Graham's Magazine* that year, Poe in a truculent mood had crossed the line and administered to *Powhatan* one of his old hatchet jobs, hardly deserved ("a more absurdly *flat* affair . . . was never before paraded to the world, with so grotesque an air of bombast and assumption," etc.). Mrs. Smith's putting aside the ill feeling that such unfair criticism might have generated says something about her emotional balance and good sense. "We harbored no malice against him," she took the trouble to say, adding that Poe as a critic "did not play with his pen, but wielded it. Right or wrong, all was real at the time. He was terribly in earnest."

As it would prove, Poe was fortunate in the woman's controlled reaction, for soon after his death she became one of his most ardent defenders, as well as one of the most penetrating. In the course of twenty years, while Poe's reputation was undergoing that fierce posthumous attack now so familiar, on three occasions she wrote lengthy articles trying to explain his restless spirit to a fascinated public. In each of the three—published in 1857, 1867, and 1876— she made reference, briefly and almost casually, to the manner of his death. What she had to say on the topic was both unexpected and not a little shocking, the three mentions becoming gradually more specific.

Mrs. Smith's first attempt to champion her friend came in the well-printed pages of the *United States Magazine.* Toward the close of the article's seven large pages offering informed discussion of his life and literary career, this occurs:

> Not long before his death he was cruelly beaten, blow upon blow, by a ruffian who knew of no better mode of avenging supposed injuries. It is well known that a brain fever followed—that he left New York precipitately—

that he reached Baltimore, the city of his nativity, and
there died on the 4th of October, 1849.

The hand should be palsied, and the name blighted, of
the man who, under any provocation, could inflict a blow
upon a slender, helpless, intellectual being, however mis-
guided, like Edgar A. Poe.

There is confusion here, of course. She misses the precise
day of Poe's death, and errs as to where the journey originated. She is also more sentimental than exact in picturing
Poe as a "helpless" intellectual. In his youth, Poe had been
an athlete of some ability and in any melee would likely
have proved himself far from helpless. That Mrs. Smith felt
able to make the statement at all, and so unequivocally, is
the salient point, reflecting the impression of him she
received.

A decade went by in which she kept up a rather fierce
writing pace, branching into novels (the popular dime pa-
perback variety), children's books, even succeeding in a
mild way in the theater. It was February 1867 before she
found the time, perhaps the inclination, to deal again with
Poe. In *Beadle's Monthly* appeared her second article, longer
than the first, and offering a still stronger defense of his
character. Again toward the end she adverts to the manner
of his dying, with one slight but telling addition:

It is asserted in the *American Cyclopedia* that Edgar Poe
died in consequence of a drunken debauch in his native
city. This is not true. At the instigation of a woman, who
considered herself injured by him, he was cruelly beaten,
blow upon blow, by a ruffian who knew no better mode
of avenging supposed injuries. It is well known that a

brain fever followed; his friends hurried him away, and he reached his native city only to breathe his last.

In her first article, in the *United States Magazine,* the beating is given a very vague causation, nothing but generalized "injuries." In *Beadle's,* though still unspecified, the injuries are linked to the feelings of an unidentified woman, with *romantic* feelings strongly implied. Whether Mrs. Smith is denying the drunken debauch in its entirety, saying it never happened, or only means to state that the death was not a direct result of the drinking, admittedly remains unclear.

Finally, in the New York *Home Journal* for March 15, 1876, Mrs. Smith's fullest development of the beating story is put into the record—fullest, yet carefully, discouragingly, strewn with gaps. She opens by enforcing the distinction between a confirmed alcoholic who never misses a day's intake, and an occasional spreer, a distinction since so familiar among Poe biographers. Also, she again denies that drink was the direct cause of death:

> That Edgar Poe may have subjected himself to the imputation of inebriety may perhaps be conceded, for a glass of wine would act fearfully upon his delicate organization; but that he was a debauched man in any way is utterly false. He was not a diseased man from his cups at the time of his death, nor did he die from *delirium tremens,* as has been asserted.
>
> The whole sad story will probably never be known, but he had corresponded freely with a woman whose name I withhold, and they having subsequently quarreled, he refused to return her letters, nor did she receive them until Dr. Griswold gave them back after Poe's death. This retention not only alarmed but exasperated the woman, and

she sent an emissary of her own to enforce the delivery, and who, failing of success, beat the unhappy man in a most ruffianly manner.

A brain fever supervened and a few friends went with him to Baltimore, his native city, which he barely reached when he died.

Long after publication of the *Home Journal* article, Mrs. Smith lived on, surviving to 1893 and dying at the advanced age of eighty-eight. In those latter years she remained active until almost the end, but never did she utter another word about Poe's death, never named her source, never hinted at the name she had chosen to withhold.

Not the least curious aspect of the Smith charge is the way it was, and has been, ignored. From Smith's day to this, no Poe biographer has given it more than a glancing look, and then only to dismiss it. The most recent discussion of the relations between Mrs. Smith and Poe hardly touches on it, tossing it off in a single sentence of denial: "Her most egregious factual error, one that she would unfortunately repeat, concerns an assault by a stranger before Poe's death in Baltimore" (of course, no "stranger" was specified by Mrs. Smith, in fact she implied that the attacker was a friend of the unnamed woman).

While Mrs. Smith lived, the idea of a physical assault on Poe was directly challenged in public on but a single occasion, and then tepidly, by Susan Talley—Mrs. Weiss— who favored a variation on the "cooping" theory. In private at the time there was also some demur, but the objection came from an old friend who had, or felt she had, some stake in Poe's reputation, Sarah Helen Whitman. What

Poe's old flame had to say on the matter does have some peculiar interest, not to say special relevance.

Of Mrs. Smith's three articles on Poe* it is certain that Mrs. Whitman had read all, and avidly. The two women were personal friends, brought together largely by a shared enthusiasm for the spiritualist movement. They kept each other informed of their writings, at times took their vacations together, the widowed Mrs. Whitman joining the Smith family, and they stayed in regular correspondence.

The first of the three articles, that in the *United States Magazine* for March 1857, brought from Mrs. Whitman a letter of comment which was quoted in the same magazine's June issue. With sharp insight, she remarks on Poe's supposedly divided or dual nature ("a divine and a demoniac"), one of the first to offer this telling observation. Mrs. Smith's article, she feels sure, will help to rid her dead friend's reputation of "some undeserved imputations."

But regarding the brutal manner of his death as it is pictured in the Smith article, his being beaten by a ruffian, she has nothing whatever to say. Neither agreement nor denial is ventured.

When the *Beadle's* article was issued, ten years later, Mrs. Whitman promptly got hold of it, but on reading it left no comment. It was only some years afterward, in a letter, that she voiced her reaction to the *Beadle's* offering, rather unexpectedly judging it to be "of no value," a strange enough reaction since it pretty much echoed what had been said in the earlier piece. Again, conspicuously, no least remark or

---

*She treats him in a fourth article, in *Baldwin's Monthly,* September 1874, but without reference to his death.

opinion is offered regarding what Mrs. Smith had to say on the manner of Poe's death.

It was with the *Home Journal* article in March 1876 that Mrs. Whitman at last began to show herself aware of the beating claim, so that she seemed to dispute it—*seemed* to. Within days of its appearance she had found and read the article, and at first was more troubled by what was said of Poe's character, his "insincerity," and his "little loves," petty amours. Within two weeks, however, after the daily papers had jumped on the beating theory, spotlighting it, Mrs. Whitman finally took notice, sparked by a brief paragraph she came across in several papers. In a letter of April 7th to the biographer Ingram she quotes the paragraph, to her both alarming and distasteful, then offers some disturbed opinions of her own:

I wonder if you have heard about a scandalous paragraph which is going the rounds of the press? This is the paragraph: "Elizabeth Oakes Smith writes in the *Home Journal* that the immediate cause of Edgar A. Poe's death was a severe beating which he received from the friend of a woman whom he had deceived and betrayed."

I have several letters denouncing Mrs. Smith for this scandalous story. Now, I do not believe that Mrs. Smith ever wrote such a paragraph or would *authorise* its insertion in any paper {she is implying that other hands were responsible for the paragraph in the Smith article: see what she says next}.

Some of the tribe of secret slanderers who are forever lying in wait for an occasion to sully his memory and obscure his fame have doubtless seized upon an idle and absurd story told by Mrs. S in that article which she wrote long ago for one of her own magazines, & which (as I think I told you in my last letter) she has lately republished in the *Home Journal*. [By "seized upon" she means rewritten and expanded from the Smith pieces.]

If you have a copy of that article you will see that her account of the cause of Poe's death has been misrepresented and misquoted, & doubtless with malign intent, by some of Poe's enemies. If I knew her present address I would write to her at once to confirm or deny this story, which is being so widely circulated under her name.

From somewhere Mrs. Whitman got hold of her friend's address, and she did write as she had promised. In her letter she expressed her firm belief that the offending paragraph had not come from Mrs. Smith, "did not emanate from her, was not written by her, not authorised by her." As promptly, Mrs. Smith replied, and "her card" of explanation was included in Mrs. Whitman's letter to Ingram. What the card said becomes clear from Ingram's response (he calls Mrs. Smith by the pet name many used for her): "I regret to say that I do not believe a single word of your imaginative friend Eva's denial of the paragraph in the *Home Journal*. I had the MS. in my own hands, in her writing, containing it! Pray be careful about accepting her denial in print. I will return her card in my next."

In this three-sided exchange, it now becomes clear, there was a thread of confusion, none of the three realizing it: they were not all talking about the same thing. But this confusion, or distortion, in itself offers considerable aid in getting at the reality.

Mild shock, or somewhat more than mild, was Mrs. Whitman's reaction to Ingram's dismaying news. Mrs.

Smith, it very much appeared, had lied to her. Immediately went off to Ingram another urgent letter of inquiry:

> Surely you do not mean to say that the paragraph stating that Poe came to his death through a brutal personal assault, "from the brothers of a woman whom he had *betrayed and ruined*"—you do not mean that the MS. of this (a brief paragraph) was, or had been in your hands? If so, all human testimony would seem questionable. She admits the story of an assault from the brothers of a woman whose letters he had declined to return, as you know, but this is *altogether a different charge.*

In that last sentence is revealed the crux of what had Mrs. Whitman so worked up, a revelation made explicit by Ingram's reply (not in itself a model of clarity):

> As to EOS, I had the MS. in my possession certainly, and certainly all, or nearly all, had been previously published by her: as to the exact words, I would not dare to assert anything, & my remarks to you referred to the *whole paper* and not to any sentence. I read your meaning that she denied authorship of the whole article. I did not notice (but will reread) "a woman whom he had *betrayed and ruined.*" I thought I had read it, "a woman whose letters he had declined etc."

It was not the beating itself, as the cause of death, that Mrs. Whitman felt so strong a need to reject. It was the *reason* assigned for the beating. She is objecting not to the beating claim, but to the charge that Poe had "betrayed and ruined" the woman in question—sexually ruined her, with "ruined" hinting at dire circumstances indeed.

So long as the causation was a mere matter of a quarrel over unreturned letters—the reason implied or stated in all three Smith articles—from Mrs. Whitman came no objection. But she would not admit to the causation having been any sort of dishonorable betrayal of female innocence. That Poe had, in some rough fashion, been manhandled by parties unknown, and that this violence led somehow to his death, she accepts without demur.

By now the confusion in the exchange may be so obvious that it needs no highlighting. The "paragraph" that Mrs. Whitman wants her friend to deny is the short one that appeared as a squib in the newspapers, not the longer one embedded in the *Home Journal* article. Ingram might eventually have grasped that fact had not Mrs. Whitman, in trying to get the emphasis right, unwittingly changed her source. In reality, in her second letter she gave the quote as it had appeared in some other paper, or other source, than the one she initially quoted. Originally, in her first letter she framed it as: "The friend of a woman whom he had deceived and betrayed." In the second letter, talking of exactly the same thing, the phrase is materially altered, becoming: "The brothers of a woman whom he had betrayed and ruined."

Brothers? Where did they come from? Whose brothers?

❦

Susan Talley, the eager young poetess who had been so impressed by Rosalie's fascinating brother, deserves to be heard regarding Poe on whatever aspect she chooses to treat—exercising due caution, as Poe biographers like to warn. During his two-month stay in Richmond that last summer no one saw more of him than Miss Talley, or enjoyed with him more unrestrained talk (of course not counting Elmira).

"I saw Poe constantly," she said later. ". . . From his sister, also, and from intimate common friends we knew all concerning him, so that about this portion of his life there is no reserve or mystery." She adds that, to her at least, the poet was never the puzzle, "the inexplicable character," he seemed to so many. Young though she was, by some instinct she had been able to discern the "finer and more elevated nature of the man."

Proudly she observes that on one occasion Poe himself commented happily, "I cannot express the pleasure—the more than pleasure—of finding myself so entirely understood by you. It is not often I am so understood."

Once the two went with a small group to visit one of the city's grand old mansions, the Hermitage, then deserted and in decay. In Poe's youth it had been the seat of the well-to-do Mayo family, and Poe had often been welcomed there as a guest. Now, strolling the grounds alongside Miss Talley, he was "unusually silent and preoccupied," a mood the young woman set down to the memories aroused. At one secluded spot in the old garden they halted and Poe recalled that white violets had once grown there. He searched among the remaining plants, found a bunch of violets and picked a few blossoms, which he "placed carefully between the leaves of a notebook." In the Hermitage itself, the big house, they strolled in silence through the empty rooms, Poe looking infinitely sad:

He passed from room to room with a grave abstracted look, and removed his hat, as if involuntarily, on entering the saloon, where in old times many a brilliant company had assembled. Seated in one of the deep windows, over which now grew masses of ivy, his memory must have borne him back to former scenes, for he repeated the familiar lines of Moore: "I feel like one who treads alone / Some banquet hall deserted . . ."

The light of the setting sun shone through the drooping ivy-boughs into the ghostly room, and the tattered and mildewed paper-hangings with their faded tracery of rose-garlands waved fitfully in the autumn breeze. An inexpressibly eerie feeling came over me which I can even now recall, and as I stood there my old childish idea of the poet as a spirit of mingled light and darkness recurred strongly to my imagination. . . .

For Susan Talley, it may be appreciated, no slightest fact about this celebrated author could come amiss or be uninteresting, this hypnotic being she saw as made up of "mingled light and darkness," and from whose dark, liquid eyes beamed an "indescribable charm, I might almost say magnetism." Hard fact and rumor, guessing and gossip, information of all kinds, known to be authentic or only supposed so, all was avidly gathered in by her, much of it to be preserved in writing, especially in her later volume, *The Home Life of Poe.* In that book, unexpectedly, she adds something about the relations between Poe and Elmira which strikes a sudden spark in the present investigation. The short interruption to their courtship, explains Talley, the situation which led Poe to take the temperance pledge, was also related to "a difficulty concerning certain letters which the lady desired to have returned to her and which he declined to give up." It was a brief but unpleasant interlude, of which Talley had personal knowledge:

Mrs. Shelton, during a few days' absence of Poe at the country home of Mr. John MacKenzie, came to Duncan Lodge and appealed to Mrs. MacKenzie to influence Poe in returning her letters. I saw her on this occasion—a tall, rather masculine-looking woman, who drew her veil over her face as she passed us on the porch, though I caught a glimpse of large, shadowy, light blue eyes which must once have been handsome. We heard no more of her until sometime about the middle of September, when suddenly Poe's visits to her were resumed. . . .

It is what she writes next in her book after that surprising mention of a quarrel over old letters that has relevance in the present case. Some seven pages afterward—and, it should be said, in no way linked to the words just quoted—expressing neither belief nor its opposite, almost offhandedly she identifies the "brothers" who were referred to in veiled terms by Mrs. Smith:

There was even a sensational story published in a northern magazine to the effect that Poe had been followed to Baltimore by two of Mrs. Shelton's brothers, and there, after having certain letters taken from him, beaten so severely that he was found dying in an obscure alley.

This story was first started by Mrs. Elizabeth Oakes Smith in one of the New York journals, though it does not appear from what source she derived her information. No denial was made or notice taken of it by Mrs. Shelton's friends, and the story gradually died out.

With that, both Mrs. Smith's article and Mrs. Shelton's brothers are dropped, never again to be mentioned by Susan Talley. In her book she goes on to offer her own idea of what happened, giving a weirdly distorted version of the "coop-ing" theory as the probable cause of Poe's death.

Of course, Mrs. Smith had nowhere identified the assail-ants as the brothers of anyone, certainly had said nothing about their being blood relatives of Elmira. In her clearest statement she refers rather guardedly to "an emissary" of the aggrieved woman, seeming to say that he was at least a friend. The notion that there might have been more than one attacker, and that they might have been Elmira's own brothers came, somewhat unexpectedly, from Susan Tal-ley—who also failed to name her source. Conspicuously, the Talley comment does not deny the charge, but instead demonstrates that it was indeed talked about in Richmond, only "gradually" dying out.

As a matter of fact, Elmira did have brothers, three of them, George, James, and Alexander Royster. In 1849 all three were living and working in Richmond. All three re-sided in the same Church Hill section as their sister. Each had a house standing no more than a block or two from the Shelton residence on Grace Street. The Roysters, it seemed, like many old Virginia families then, formed an unusually close-knit group, even to clannishness.

If only Elizabeth Smith had thought to leave on record some hint about her authority for the beating charge, her source. But she didn't, not a syllable. It should be added, however, that she did enjoy especially close contacts in Richmond circles, both social and professional. She was particularly intimate with one Richmond family, that of Thomas White, first proprietor of *The Southern Literary Mes-senger* when it was being edited by Poe. Years later, in fact,

White's daughter Eliza went north to live for a time with the Smiths.

Then Susan Talley—if only *she* had thought to say something more beyond a casual mention of Elmira's brothers as Poe's attackers. She didn't—but here again it should be recalled that she was a lifelong resident of Richmond, enjoying ties of blood and friendship with many of the city's old families.

With no further clues on hand, no direct evidence, to bridge the gap between charge and reality, the investigation at last begins to stall. However, one slight opening does present itself, and that is the undoubted fact that both these women had *heard* something. Both had been told something, by some person or persons unknown. The alternative, that the two had simply dreamed up what they wrote, is not at all tenable. To make so firm a statement so publicly, Mrs. Smith must have believed strongly in her source. Similarly with Susan Talley. While she didn't assert an attack on Poe, she certainly did reflect the existence of such talk.

The point of origin for Susan Talley's information would unquestionably have been the city of Richmond itself, so the question may be posed: who in Richmond might have known the truth, or what was believed to be the truth? The question, in its grasping at likelihood, is perhaps too sweeping. Yet as it turns out, it *can* be answered, and by merely putting one final query: who in Richmond, then or at any later time, ventured to offer public comment or remark on the *manner* of Poe's death—not simply lamenting its occurrence but making precise observations as to the *how* and the *why?*

There was only one such party, the then editor of the *Messenger,* John R. Thompson, the very man who had originated the "cooping" theory.

A good deal of Poe's time while he was in Richmond, it is known, was spent in Thompson's *Messenger* office. He made it his professional headquarters, and precisely at Thompson's own kind invitation. Flattered to make even a temporary crony of the famous poet, Thompson spent much time discussing with him such matters as the sorry condition of the magazine business, and the state of American writing and authorship in general, also arranging for new contributions to the *Messenger* pages by Poe. However, Thompson was not an uncritical admirer of his guest. His personal view of him, in fact, was downright ambivalent.

Thompson did tend to picture Poe as the typical Romantic poet, perpetually lost in what he called "dreamy abstraction," always wandering hazily in "the shadowy realm of ideas." But he could never quite overlook or forget or forgive the drinking, a habit which, for Thompson, cancelled all redeeming qualities. It was, he wrote, "impossible to consider him apart from the melancholy propensity which tended to make his life miserable."

Even beyond the drinking, Thompson could not accept his friend and colleague as entirely worthy: "He had extraordinary genius, but he lacked sympathy; he was not selfish, but he did not enter warmly into the affairs of others who were ready to befriend him; he was capable of generous and chivalrous actions, but a wayward impulse made him neglectful of the inexorable duties of life."

Another time he went further, actually defending as true and accurate the harshly damning portrait of Poe drawn by

Rufus Griswold in his obituary, and later in that badly distorted *Memoir*. Griswold, he conceded, had written "some hard things of his subject," but suppression of the facts would have been dishonest. "Kindness to the dead," states Thompson, "indeed requires that we should deal tenderly with their reputations, but there are some cases in which a too-great fastidiousness would be positive injustice to the living." Thompson may have been much impressed by Poe as a writer. For the man personally he had little use.

For present purposes, the significant thing, the relevant point regarding John Thompson is the very curious fact that his "cooping" theory was an afterthought. Only when Mrs. Smith had put forward her beating charge did the cooping idea make its appearance.

At first, Thompson accepted Poe's death, as did everyone then, as the result of a drunken debauch, indulged in that fatal one time too many. Scarcely a month afterward he is heard saying in a letter that Poe "died, indeed, of delirium from drunkenness; the shadow of infamy beclouded his last moments." Ten years later he is heard saying the same thing, this time to the actress-author Anna Mowatt, who mentioned it in a letter she wrote in the summer of 1859: Poe, said Thompson, had "an attack of delirium, was carried to a hospital and died there."

Not until the late 1860s, some few years after the conclusion of the Civil War (in his lecture he refers to "the recent war"), did he come out with his cooping theory. By no means tentative, he postulated the theory in downright terms that left little room for disagreement: "seized by the lawless agents of a political club, imprisoned in a cellar for the night, and taken out next morning in a state bordering on frenzy," etc. By then, Mrs. Smith had twice stated her own belief in Poe's having been beaten to death by ruffians who were related to, or agents of, some offended woman.

When Mrs. Smith's first effort came out, in the *United States Magazine,* in March 1857, Thompson was in Europe on an extended visit. When her second effort made its appearance, in *Beadle's* for February 1867, he was back in America in the thick of things, working in New York as literary editor for the *Evening Post.* It was now, twenty years after the fact, that he formed his idea of violent election mobs being responsible for the poet's death.

Put into broad, public circulation through Stoddard in *Harper's Magazine,* snapped up by the group of journalists in Baltimore that gathered around William Hand Browne and his *Southern Magazine,* the new theory soon gained credence among Poe adherents. In magazine articles and the first Poe biographies (Gill, Ingram, Harrison, Woodbury, to name the foremost), it was soberly recounted, expanding at each repetition until it came to seem by far the most probable solution. Meantime, Mrs. Smith's assertion about deliberate violence committed on Poe by individual attackers was allowed to fade quietly away.

Did John Thompson have a personal acquaintance with the Royster family? With the Royster brothers? With the Sheltons? Did he try, going to some lengths, to protect the Royster men by diverting suspicion from them with his cleverly conceived "cooping" theory?

Given Thompson's position in Richmond, and his close association with Poe that summer, it is quite likely that he did know both the Sheltons and the Roysters, Elmira and her brothers. (A sometime colleague of his, Edward Alfriend, who took over as editor of the *Messenger* after

Thompson departed, had long been on social terms with the Sheltons.) In the spring of 1873, just before the start of interest in serious Poe biography, he died of consumption at the age of fifty in New York City. His body was returned to Richmond for burial.

❦

If George, James, and Alexander Royster, the loving brothers of Elmira Shelton, had in fact vowed to prevent their wealthy but lonely sister from marrying a man they condemned as a ruthless fortune hunter and profligate, how would they have accomplished their grim purpose?

From that question comes another, even more pertinent: if the three brothers did have a direct hand in Poe's death, how did the tragedy happen to play itself out in a *Baltimore* tavern, a *Baltimore* hospital? *There* is the necessary starting point, for as the evidence demonstrates, Poe's travels had already carried him well beyond the confines of that city.

Heading north on his fatal journey, Poe passed through Baltimore, and then reached Philadelphia, where he was aided by Sartain and Lippard. Yet when found he was back again in Baltimore. In that unexplained return nestles the one indispensible clue, sought for so long in vain, even while it lay in plain sight (curiously supporting Poe's dictum in *The Purloined Letter* about *the obvious* often affording the best concealment).

What follows is the whole sad story of Poe's untimely end as it takes shape in the view of one investigator after long and careful pondering. Told in sequence and with only needed halts for analysis, it rests squarely on established fact as recorded in the foregoing pages, and sober inference from those facts.

❨ 8 ❩

Suddenly a Tapping

aking his arm, Elmira pushed back the coat sleeve and felt Poe's pulse. It seemed a bit fast and the skin was rather warm to the touch. On his broad, pale forehead she placed her palm, and decided that it, too, felt hot. Answering her question, he admitted feeling unwell, though naming no special complaint.

Concerned that he might be coming down with something, she asked if he really had to leave on the morning steamer for the north as planned. Why not wait a day or two? No, Poe replied, his appointment with Mrs. Loud in Philadelphia was for Thursday evening. The morning boat, followed by the six-hour train ride, would get him to the Loud house with little time to spare. It was an important commission, a hundred dollars for very little work. He didn't want to risk it, not now with their marriage looming so close. He'd be feeling all right soon enough, he finished.

The two bade each other farewell, and said how they looked forward to meeting again in two weeks. After that, there would be only one additional week to wait before the wedding, since the ceremony had been set for October 17th, beginning for both a wonderful new life. Think of it! More than twenty years after the breaking of their youthful engagement they would finally be united! In their hearts it seemed almost like a miracle, a resurrection— for Elmira the end of loneliness, for Poe a halt to rootless wandering.

As he descended the front steps of Elmira's house on Grace Street and walked off into the night, behind him as the door swung shut he heard Elmira's last soft goodby.

Happy to be on his way, he still couldn't help feeling a deep concern. The engagement was barely a month old and already he was facing trouble. Several of Elmira's relatives had spoken out against the marriage, and there was the blatant rejection and resentment displayed by the two Shelton children, Ann and Southall. Not at all a pleasant prospect, the need to convince people that there was nothing to fear from him, that he was determined to behave, to control his drinking, and make the marriage work.

Winning over the two children would involve its own special problems, of course. But he would deal with that himself, and had already decided to become their tutor, thus exposing them to his affable side. When he really wanted to, he could capture the affections of anyone, youngsters in particular.

Elmira's three brothers might prove somewhat harder to handle. They had not been at all backward about offering their opinions on the match, a sharply negative one. To Poe, directly, they'd said nothing about how they felt—Elmira wouldn't have stood for that—but they weren't shy about speaking to others, causing talk that wound its way back to Poe. About the reasons for their opposition there was no mystery. He was all too well aware of the reasons, the tattered reputation that had dogged him up north concerning his relations with so many different women, a reputation that had inevitably filtered south. There was also his plan, all too obvious, to use Elmira's money for his magazine, and no doubt for his personal benefit as well.

Then there was his drinking, always his drinking. That problem, at least, he felt sure he'd put behind him when he joined the Sons of Temperance. From the way the papers reported the move, everyone in Richmond must be aware of it!

It was a little after nine p.m. on September 26th when Poe exited the house on Grace Street. Deliberately, he had postponed his supper, saving it to occupy him while he awaited the early morning boat. Sadler's Restaurant, his usual resort when out, was a walk of fifteen minutes from Elmira's place, a dozen blocks. As he headed for it along Grace Street, he decided that he would first see if the office of Dr. Carter was still open. Maybe he could get something to speed his recovery. It lay in the same direction, also about fifteen minutes distant from Elmira's, and a block to the north, at 17th and Broad. The walk down to Sadler's place from Carter's office would add only another five minutes or so to his journey.

"I had not seen Poe for some days," testified Carter, "when one evening about half-past nine he called at my office." Why the office was open so late, Carter didn't say, nor did he recall that Poe's specific reason for going there was to procure medicine. He remembered only that his visitor's stay was a short one, and that while the two talked, Poe sat "playing with" the doctor's new sword-cane. Repeatedly he drew the shining blade from the slim scabbard and flourished it playfully in the air (that seems the only adequate description of Carter's phrase).

When he left the office after some twenty minutes, without a word to Carter he took the sword-cane with him, leaving his own cane behind.

Lately, he'd felt quite restless, uneasy, even at times apprehensive. All the ugly and unreasonable opposition to his coming marriage had worn away some of his old self-confidence—the sudden and surprisingly cold attitudes of some, the innuendo and the whispered hints that the marriage might never take place, the dark looks of the Royster brothers whenever he encountered them at Elmira's or elsewhere. Even the fierce dislike of him shown by the two Shelton children, which seemed to speak of coaching by adults. ("They wept and pleaded with their mother not to marry Mr. Poe," and Ann, even when an old woman would become "incensed" at the mere linking of her mother's name with that of the poet.) Just on instinct, nothing more, he felt safer having a weapon, a concealed one, in his hand. If he'd *asked* for the loan of the sword-cane, of course, he wouldn't have known how to explain things.

It was not quite ten o'clock when Poe pushed through the doors of Sadler's Restaurant, at the corner of 16th and Main. To his table as he ate came the proprietor, glad to have the patronage of the renowned author, and the two were joined for a while by J. M. Blakey, the owner of the Swan Tavern, where Poe was then staying. A leisurely two hours passed, during which other acquaintances came up to say hello. When Poe departed he was "in good spirits and sober," according to Sadler.

The Baltimore boat left from Rockett's Landing every morning at five-thirty. A vessel of the United States Line, official carrier of the southern mails, it departed on schedule, and passengers were advised to be on board at least an hour prior to sailing (those who wished could board earlier and catch a few hours' sleep in the narrow dormitory bunks). Reaching Hampton Roads, off Norfolk, by three in the afternoon, passengers were transferred to one of the big bay steamers for the overnight run up to Baltimore. On both legs of the trip hot meals were served, and on the bay boats small cabins were available, all covered by the single fare of six dollars, one way.

Arrival in Baltimore was scheduled for six the next morning, September 28th, and mostly the boats were on time. Making the trip much faster were the trains, but they were uncomfortable and cost more than twice as much. A leisurely progress down the lovely James River and then up majestic Chesapeake Bay was worth the added time.

From Sadler's, Poe walked back to his room at the Swan, some twenty minutes away on foot, at the corner of 9th and Broad streets. By one o'clock, or soon after, he had finished packing his trunk for the trip, leaving his valise with some unwanted items in storage at the Swan to await his return (the trunk, a small one, would be handier coming back). Two hours remained before he'd need to leave for Rockett's, but he'd decided to go aboard early.

Handing in his room key at the desk, he was not aware that he had forgotten to take the sword-cane. Next day it would be found in his room and eventually would make its way back to Dr. Carter. Before many hours had passed, Poe would wish fervently that he had it with him, or something like it.

When at five-thirty the boat's lines were cast off, and the vessel under low steam inched its way into the river's main channel, Poe felt very glad to be on his way, eager to complete his various tasks in Philadelphia and up north and return. Had he known what was happening behind the scenes he would have been in a far different frame of mind, for on leaving the Swan he'd been followed. As he boarded the boat, three pairs of eyes watched him warily from the shadows of the wharf. Just before the vessel departed one of the three pursuers went quietly aboard.

When the boat moved out from Rockett's, picking up speed downriver, the other two pursuers hurried to the railway station, where a little later they climbed aboard the Baltimore train.

It was about six a.m. next morning when Poe debarked at the Light Street dock in Baltimore. From there he would proceed by rail to Philadelphia, a ride of some six hours. The train, however, didn't leave until nine that morning. This gave time enough to reach Mrs. Loud by midafternoon, but it burdened him with three empty hours of waiting in Baltimore. As one persistent but unverifiable tradition insists, he may have called at the office of an old acquaintance, Dr. Nathan Brooks, still perhaps seeking medication. If he did, he found that Brooks was absent.

Well before the nine a.m. departure, Poe was seated aboard the Philadelphia train, still unaware that he was being followed. His pursuers, careful not to be spotted, watched closely as he boarded, noted where he sat, then themselves took seats in other cars, behind and ahead of his.

For six hours and more the train rumbled and lurched its way north, passing through or stopping briefly in one small town after another, halting for a longer period at Wilmington, then settling into the last stretch up along the shore of the Delaware River. At about three o'clock in the afternoon it reached the outskirts of Philadelphia and minutes later chugged into the main depot on Market Street.

For what happened next, immediately on arrival and for the ensuing twenty-four hours, no specific clue points the way. Yet here probability—*strong* probability, to be sure, amounting almost to certainty—confidently fills the gap.

Prior to calling at the house of the Louds to fulfill his editorial commission, Poe took a room at a nearby hotel (perhaps the United States Hotel, not far from the station). Tired from his slow, bumpy ride, sooty from the clouds of flying cinders spewed out all along the way by the tiny locomotive's huge funnel, he was looking forward to a wash and an hour's rest. But before he had a chance to settle down, on the door of his chamber there sounded a gentle tapping. Answering it, he pulled the door wide, expecting to see a bellboy carrying a message.

Instead, he was surprised to find himself staring into the familiar but now darkly stern faces of three men, Elmira's brothers. Roughly they crowded in on him, shoving him back and shutting the door. They came right to the point.

In threatening tones they told him that his marriage to their sister must not take place. They would not allow it. Duped as she was, they would not permit Elmira to throw her life away on a money-chasing, womanizing drunkard. They had heard all those stories about his disgraceful behavior up north, they were in touch with people in New

York and Boston, people who were all too aware of his transgressions. They knew all about his fathering of a bastard child.

They weren't there to discuss the matter with him, they ended. They'd come after him for the sole purpose of warning him off, to make him understand that the marriage *must not* happen. No hint of this meeting, they instructed, must get back to their sister, or to anyone else in Richmond. That's why they had taken the trouble to get well away from home before confronting him. He was to continue on to New York, they directed harshly, *and not return.* If he did try to come back they would not hesitate to use drastic measures to ensure their sister's safety and happiness, *very* drastic. They would be watching, they finished, to see that he went on to New York by the next train. No excuses, no delays for any reason—he was to leave by the *next* train and not come back.

How the shocked Poe managed to escape from the room and from the hotel, eluding his angry pursuers, is also a matter of conjecture. Any number of clever shifts and ruses may be imagined, and in the absence of all indication, the reader must make the choice, taking into account the need for the Roysters to be quietly discreet in such a busy public place. One or two of the three must have stayed in the room with him, so his escape would have had in it some element of luck. But that he did get away is shown by his hectic descent on Sartain at his place of business. "Early one Monday afternoon," testified Sartain, "he suddenly made his appearance in my engraving-room, looking pale and haggard and with a wild expression in his eyes." He urgently needed a place to hide, explained the agitated visitor, and he proceeded to tell of being followed by threatening, un-named men.*

Since Poe would hardly have told his protector the full truth in such a matter, the details of his account, as it was later supplied by Sartain, are not all germane. Still, Poe did, it appears, make one slip, not being quick enough in his disturbed condition to think up a good cover story.

Why on earth would anyone want to kill him? asked the seriously puzzled Sartain.

"It was for revenge," blurted Poe, taken off guard and naming the first reason that leaped to mind.

"Revenge for what?" inquired Sartain, even more per-plexed. What could Poe possibly have done to deserve kill-ing, he asked himself, feeling at a loss.

"Well, a woman trouble," was the mumbled reply, Poe regretting instantly his too-honest answer, and thankful that Sartain was gentleman enough not to press the point.

Here, unmistakably, is the sudden bright glare of reality, for in this brief exchange lurks one of the more revealing aspects of the whole Sartain episode. Poe's reluctant admis-sion that "a woman" was behind his anxious fear is quite enough in itself to show that the incident did *not* take place in the summer of 1849, as is supposed. That July, he was not involved with *any* woman—he had broken with Helen Whitman fully six months before, and hadn't yet taken up with Elmira. In July there simply wasn't any woman play-ing an active, personal role in his life, so as to cause such dire complications. Beyond doubt, the phrase "a woman

---

* If Sartain was correct as to the day of the week, then it would have been October 1st. More probably, it was Friday, September 28th, or the next day. At that time, Sartain might easily have been at work on a Saturday.

trouble" was uttered by the disturbed poet not in July, but in September, when in flight from his pursuers, Mrs. Shelton's brothers. It is surprising, of course, that he admitted even this much, and the reason he did so can be linked to his intense excitement, what Sartain referred to as his all-too-apparent "mental overstrain."

But shelter from pursuers wasn't Poe's only goal in fleeing to the good-hearted Sartain. As the engraver made clear, he wanted help in disguising his appearance, and *that* interesting fact is enough to indicate what happened next, that is, to account for Poe's presence back in Baltimore after having just passed through that city on his way north.

In desperation, fiercely determined not to surrender what seemed his last chance for a more normal life, he was making a headlong dash *through* Baltimore, bound for Richmond, hoping to reach the house on Grace Street. Once back with Elmira, he told himself fervently, the nightmare would be over and all would be made right. She would call off her savage brothers. She would forbid them ever again to interfere in her personal affairs. He *must* get back to Elmira!

With Sartain he didn't remain long, only overnight, it may be, or for two nights. Then, with his moustache scissored off by his friend ("until he was absolutely barefaced"), he slipped round to one of the city's secondhand clothing stores, many of which could be found at the town center.

Discarding his own well-tailored suit of fine, black broadcloth, he hurriedly donned a motley assortment of replacements: ill-fitting pants of common, grayish cassimere, and a baggy coat of ordinary thin alpaca. Slipping out of his shining black boots, he shoved his feet into a pair of ordinary workman's shoes. His own fancy, collared vest he flung aside, also tearing off his flowing neckcloth. On his head he jammed a bedraggled old palm-leaf hat, stripped of the usual colorful broad band, its brim hanging limp and uneven.

Looking the part of any down-and-outer on the city streets, he crept warily out of the store, heading for the office of George Lippard, near the train station. In on top of the busy editor he barged suddenly, again, as with Sartain, seeking shelter. Until he could make it to the railway depot he needed a safe place to hide. To the surprised Lippard, of course, he told a different story, though the need for money was probably true enough.

If the stay in Philadelphia covered, say, three nights— two with Sartain and one with Lippard—then Poe was back in Baltimore by October 1st. From there, for the run down to Richmond, he would surely have intended to take the train rather than the boat, the train being much the faster.

He never made it. In Philadelphia the three Roysters had not been thrown completely off the track, not for long. On the return train to Baltimore they were aboard, hovering near, ready when the situation allowed to pounce.

❦

A medically qualified observer has suggested—without accusing anyone—that Poe actually died from the effects of a severe head injury. He described it in professional terms as "intracerebral trauma," leading to "epidural hematoma," a brain hemhorrage. Whether the damage resulted from a deliberate blow at the hands of an attacker, or from a drunken fall in the street in which the unfortunate man struck his head on the pavement, isn't discussed.

On the question of a physical attack, the only firsthand testimony, more or less direct, was supplied by Dr. Snodgrass in his second article. Taking issue with Mrs. Smith's claim about a beating ("As an isolated fact the probabilities do not sustain it"), he declares that he spotted no sign of rough handling:

> I am positive that there was no evidence whatever of any such violence having been used upon his person, when I went to his rescue at the tavern. Nor was there any given at the hospital, where its detection would have been certain, if external violence had really been the cause of his insanity, for there would have been some physical traces of it on the patient's person. In this view of the question I respectfully submit that it is high time that the hypothesis of a beating were dropped.

Whether Snodgrass at the hospital was able to inspect Poe unclothed, or whether he received a specific report on the question from Dr. Moran, goes unmentioned. Without either of these, his witness as to the absence of observable injury is confined to the head, face, and hands, and the state of the clothing (he does note that the alpaca coat had "ripped seams" and was "soiled," but these defects might have been sustained at any time). Dr. Moran in his early letter to Mrs. Clemm has no reference to outward physical injury, so it may be said that, in a way, he corroborates Snodgrass. If such injuries were unmistakably present, probably he would have mentioned them in his letter.

Still, none of this is conclusive, so the question must be posed: did George, James, and Alexander Royster, on catching up with the despised Poe in Baltimore, to enforce their prohibition on his returning to Richmond, subject him to physical abuse? Did they beat him? Did that beating somehow result in his death?

If they did *not* beat him, what then *did* they do to put a definite end to their sister's marriage plans? How did they save her from what they viewed as looming disaster, a fate it seemed to be their personal responsibility as the men of the family to prevent? The answer lies, partly, in the fact that Poe when found was far gone in drink. It also lies, partly, in how he got that way.

If the train from Philadelphia had pulled into Baltimore in time to connect with the train for Richmond, all might have been well. If Poe hadn't bothered about getting his trunk (full of valuable manuscripts and annotated books) and having it carried to the hotel, if he'd lingered in the crowd at the depot instead of hurrying over to the Bradshaw Hotel—thinking it would be safer to wait in seclusion—things might still have worked out. But the trains didn't connect, he did go after his trunk, did take a room at the hotel—and his doom was sealed.

As he left the depot, the three brothers trailed him, watching as he checked in at the hotel. Scarcely had he settled in his room when they again barged in. First came a faint tap on the locked door, then in response to Poe's wary question perhaps a polite, "Message, sir." As the door opened a crack there came a sudden rush into the room.

This time the brothers were ready to act, to take the drastic step they'd threatened. But it was not mere physical chastisement they administered. A simple beating, they well understood, with someone of Poe's character, might not prove a sufficient deterrent. Unwrapping a package, they produced a large bottle of whiskey. Then, holding the struggling Poe down, they forced him to break his month-old pledge never again to touch liquor, the pledge that had been so widely reported in the press. The one indispensible condition insisted on by Elmira for her marriage to Poe, they knew, was sobriety, complete and permanent. If word reached her that he had again indulged in one of his disgusting old flings, openly in public, all thought of marriage would be at an end.

But before carrying out their awful plan they went another wily step further—so I conclude—warning him never to tell anyone about their encounter. To drive home and enforce their command they added a threat that if he revealed what had been done to him they would create a major scandal in Richmond, reducing to shreds any reputation he might have left. They would bring to the surface, informing the newspapers, all the rumors about his vile conduct up north, his fathering of an illegitimate child with the poetess Fanny Osgood, as well as that very ugly business of his deliberate break with the trusting Mrs. Whitman. Whether these rumors were true didn't matter to them. The rumors were already in circulation, and the Roysters would see to it that the Richmond papers picked them up. It would not be hard to do, getting such stories into print, carefully phrased, with just enough detail and innuendo to make the charges plain, and unmistakable as to who was involved.

In a sudden fit of anger Poe at last erupted. Wildly he charged his tormenters, fists flailing, as he tried to fight his way out of the room. It was in the resulting melee, probably, that he did receive some hard blows, perhaps even to the head. But the odds were against him. Overpowered by the three, he was backed down into a chair. While two of the brothers pinned his arms, the third pressed the mouth of the open bottle to his grimly clamped lips. Sputtering and choking, resisting fiercely, he gradually weakened and was soon swallowing surge after surge of the fiery liquid.

An hour, perhaps, was needed to get him to just the right pitch. Then they lifted him to his feet and escorted him out of the hotel, down a few streets, and into a public bar. There, slumped at a table, they left him. Now he'd go on drinking until he was paralyzed, they knew, likely would attract attention by causing some havoc. An anonymous tip to the Baltimore newspapers would do the rest. The bar to which they took him, chosen at random, was Ryan's Tavern, located in Gunner's Hall, ten or so blocks from the Bradshaw (perhaps they used a cab).

It was late on Tuesday, October 2nd, when the Roysters deposited the staggering Poe at Ryan's place. That night when the bar closed he was put out along with the other drunks. Through the long, dark hours that followed, and through much of the next morning, he lay stretched half-conscious on a wooden plank in a nearby alley.

At last he struggled up and stumbled back to Ryan's, looking for more drink. But it was election day and the bar was closed. Into a chair he slumped, sodden and weary, only half aware of the shuffling feet and the noisy talk of the voters swirling around him. Then someone, some man, was leaning over him, asking his name, asking if he knew anyone in town who might wish to help him.

Barely was he able to pronounce the name of Dr. Snodgrass.

※

In the hospital at first—during a period of no less than ten hours, according to Dr. Moran—Poe remained in a restless, somnolent state, feverish and perspiring heavily.

Now and then able to respond feebly to questions, his replies were mostly unintelligible, nor could he recall anything that had happened to him. By noon the next day, October 4th, he had slipped into "a violent delirium," talking aloud to and about "objects on the walls."

This went on for another twenty hours, when finally toward evening on the 5th he calmed down and seemed on his way to recovery. But Dr. Moran, on talking with him, found that he was still badly fuddled.

Personal questions put to him by the doctor about his family, his relatives, where he lived, where he'd come from and was going, what had become of his luggage, brought only a stream of "incoherent" responses. The one statement that came clearly from the parched lips concerned Elmira: to Moran, he insisted that "he had a wife in Richmond." Better than any other single item, that pathetic misstatement shows what was still uppermost on his clouded mind—the urgent need to reach the woman who alone could save the awful situation.

Thoughts of Elmira also seemed reflected in his bitter remark to Moran about his friends. The best thing any friend could do for him, he murmured savagely, would be to take a pistol and "blow out his brains!" Even if dimly in his blurred confusion, he feared that for him it was all over. He had lost Elmira.

Unexpectedly, just as he appeared to be on the mend, the delirium again gripped him, and this time more violently. Physically weakened as he was, in his wild raving it still took two nurses to keep him prostrate in his bed. By Saturday night he'd become loudly vocal once more, among other things repeatedly calling out what sounded like the name "Reynolds." No one has ever succeeded in explaining who this may have been, or why the name so occupied the fevered brain, if indeed it was a name and not some other word. Much speculation has been ventured on the point, all of it with a literary background, none of it very convincing.

Even now, to the little mystery there can be added only one new fact, small but rather interesting. As newspapers of the day record, at Ryan's Fourth Ward polls in Gunner's Hall on election day, one of the three presiding judges was a man who bore the name of Henry R. Reynolds. Present in the same room as Poe on October 3rd at Ryan's place, only days before he began in his delirium to call out the name, was an actual, flesh-and-blood Reynolds. The coincidence suggests, at least, that there may have been no real significance at all to the name as it was mouthed by the dying poet. Delirium is not a rational process. The sodden brain may simply have picked up a sound it heard spoken in the haze of the noisy room, sparking some far-drawn memory . . .

Reynolds . . . Reynolds . . . Jeremiah Reynolds, pioneer explorer of the South seas . . . Jeremiah Reynolds, inspirer of Poe's story about Arthur Gordon Pym's adventures "still farther south" into unknown regions of the Antarctic . . . Pym's own final, mysterious end coming as the helpless ship is caught in a raging tide, while ahead a strange "luminous glare" begins to tint the misty darkness. . . . "And now we rushed into the embraces of the cataract, where a chasm threw itself open to receive us. But there arose in our pathway a shrouded human figure, very far larger in its proportions than any dweller among men. And the hue of the skin of the figure was of the perfect whiteness of the snow" . . . and the story ends.

With that, following an abrupt turn for the worse that was particularly noted by Neilson Poe, death came swiftly. After a visit to his cousin at the hospital on the 4th or 5th, Neilson came away feeling happily that the worst was over, and that the recovery had begun. "I was never so shocked in my life," he wrote Mrs. Clemm afterward, "as when, on Sunday morning, notice was sent to me that he was dead." Beyond whatever physiological failure was involved in the sudden reversal, certainly contributing to it was Poe's own despair, his sense of utter hopelessness.

As dawn broke on Sunday, October 7th, the patient's excitement slowly receded, then passed off. Stretched silent and unmoving on the bed, for another two hours Poe lay quiet, eyes mostly closed, now and then opening to stare blankly at the ceiling. Hovering round the bed, the nurses watched closely.

At length the head with its dark, matted hair moved slightly, swaying gently and repeatedly from side to side. From the barely moving lips came a murmur of something that the nurses reported as "God help my poor soul."

The two women bent over the prostrate figure and found that his breathing had stopped.

Epilogue

Exit the Widow

hocked almost beyond expression at the news of her fiancé's sudden death, Elmira barely managed to pour "the horrible truth," as she called it, into a long letter to Mrs. Clemm written two days after the awful fact reached her in the columns of the *Whig.*

Her lost love, she moans "was the *dearest object* on earth to me!" and she confesses that the pleasure she had anticipated "on his return with you, dear friend! to Richmond, was too great ever to be realized." This overwhelming disappointment, she finishes hopelessly, would teach her "the folly of expecting bliss on earth."

In closing her letter she assures Poe's mother-in-law of her continued solicitude, and begs the woman to write immediately: "let me hear from you, as I shall be anxious about you incessantly until I do."

Elmira's concern for the welfare of Mrs. Clemm, now left

nearly destitute, certainly was genuine when uttered, as was her woe and dismay over the loss of the man she loved. Yet it was soon afterward, *very* soon afterward, that she began to withdraw from all association with Mrs. Clemm, and from everything connected in any way with Poe. For the next twenty-five years, still living as a widow in or near Richmond, while interest in her famous fiancé boiled through the press in article after article, Elmira bluntly refused all requests for information about him. Literally to no one would she speak on the topic of Poe, not about his character, his personality, his work. One of her few surviving letters, written in 1852, shows her gracefully but firmly refusing such a request. She "would beg to be excused from communicating anything which might bring me before the public in any form whatever."

Alone of all the women who had been close to him, Elmira did *not* claim that Poe had written any verses to or about her. Always she vehemently denied the growing tradition in her native city that she, and no other, was the lost Lenore of *The Raven,* or had been the inspiration for the limpid lines of *Annabel Lee.*

Not until 1875 did she break her self-imposed silence, speaking briefly with a local acquaintance, sculptor Edward Valentine, who approached her on behalf of biographer John Ingram. Then for another dozen years she again drew back, uttering not a word more. When she died, on February 11, 1888, aged seventy-eight, the obituary in the *Whig* referred to her as "Poe's first and last love," and took special note of her long silence concerning "the passionate and dark-eyed man" she had so nearly married.

What prompted her to open up, the one time that she did, was something that Ingram himself had written, something he had included in his first preliminary sketch of the poet in 1874. Her apparent reason for speaking out was as surprising as it was sudden: she wished to go on record as denying that she had ever been engaged to Poe, denying as well the widespread rumor that she had, on Poe's death, dressed in public mourning.

Valentine's initial contact with Elmira—made in the fall of 1874, well before she could have read the Ingram sketch—actually shows her *refusing* him. Her short note of reply to his inquiry still exists and in it she coolly states that she is "not prepared" to supply any information on Poe. "There are many others," she remarks, "who profess to know much more than I do." Along with her own note she carefully returned Valentine's letter of inquiry.

In the following year, however, sometime in the spring, she read Ingram's sketch and was disturbed to find her name for the first time made public (prior references had been to "a lady of Richmond," or to "a wealthy widow"). Poe, wrote Ingram, had not been long in Richmond on his final visit, "before it was rumored that he was engaged to the love of his youth, Mrs. Shelton, who was now a widow. . . . there would appear to have been some truth in the report, and on the news of Poe's death Mrs. Shelton went into mourning for him."

To this statement Elmira's response was both prompt and revealingly indirect. Through mutual friends, taking care to make it all appear casual, she sent Valentine word that the biographer was wrong on both counts, information that Valentine immediately passed to Ingram. "I heard on Saturday night," wrote Valentine on July 20, 1875, "that Mrs. Shelton says that you are mistaken in some statements in your account of Poe. She says that she did not wear mourning after his death and also, I think, that she was not engaged to him at the time of his death. But I will try and find out more positively about this."

It took Elmira another three months to agree to a face-to-face interview, and the impetus this time certainly was the news that Ingram had begun work on a full-scale biography of the poet. On the afternoon of November 19, 1875 Elmira met with Valentine at the home of one of her friends in town. Judging by the interviewer's jumbled notes as he wrote them up afterward, the meeting was a short one, as little as fifteen minutes, not nearly so much as a half-hour.

Again, Elmira's main concern was with making an absolute denial of any formal commitment of herself to Poe. Threaded through her brief answers to Valentine's questions are some quite decided statements on exactly that point, softening just a bit as the interview reached its end:

> I did not put on a particle of mourning for him . . . he entreated me to marry him, implored me, and it was distressing to see how he implored me . . . I told him if he would not take a positive denial he must give me time to consider of it . . . I never engaged myself to him. He begged me when he was going away to marry him, promised he would be everything I could desire . . . I was not engaged to Poe when he left here, but there was a partial understanding, but I do not think I should have married him under any circumstances . . .

In her persistent quest to unlink herself from any too-close association with Poe—in the process, of course, shielding her three brothers, surely the main purpose of all her dissembling—the widow succeeded rather well. Not only in her own time, but clear up to the present she was able to cloud the issue.

Of Elmira in his 1880 biography Ingram wrote that, while there may have been some sort of understanding between them, she "does not appear to have definitely engaged herself to Poe." Today, that same vagueness, that wavering indecision regarding the affair have worked themselves permanently in the fabric of Poe's life story. *Were* the two engaged or weren't they, asks one authority after another, and the disagreement goes on and the question is never settled.

But there is one witness who, if granted a hearing, might have all but settled the question a century ago. That witness, however, was Dr. John Moran, who had managed to disqualify himself, losing all favor with Poe scholars impatient over his later distortions and his silly exaggerations concerning Poe's final hours. That was unfortunate, for Moran did perform one last chore of value which has ever since been ignored. In June 1884, as Elmira entered her seventy-fifth year, he went to call on her at her home in Richmond. For a long time she had hoped to see and talk with the physician who had been at the dying poet's bedside. Now she had her wish, but in the emotional, four-hour talk she suddenly broke down. In a rush of feeling she admitted everything, confessing to "the strength of the attachment" between herself and Poe, "in plain words, how much they loved." Yes, she told her visitor, there had indeed been a formal engagement. With that, "the venerable lady put her handkerchief to her face and wept."

Of Elmira's brothers there is little more that can be said. Despite their burden of guilt, presumably they went on to live normal, happy lives, then like most people faded into history (George and James are listed in Richmond directories through the 1890s). What may have been their last move in the tragedy came when they prevailed on their sister—so I judge—to inquire about the one thing beyond their control—whether Poe in the hospital had said anything about them. To Dr. Moran, Elmira wrote directly, asking specifically if his delirious patient had experienced any lucid intervals. "I write to you to learn from you, as his physician," she stated, "particulars in regard to his illness, disease, and how he died, whether conscious at any time previous to his demise or not."

Moran's reply is missing, but it would have repeated the information he had earlier supplied to Mrs. Clemm: at moments Poe had been tranquil, but his rambling talk had never been more than incoherent. The Royster-Shelton clan could rest secure, confident that the dying poet had whispered no final accusation.

It may well be that in acting as they did, the Royster brothers in fact preserved their sister from the tragedy of a disastrous marriage. Perhaps their brutal interference really did spare Elmira a future full of worry and distraction, if nothing worse.

But is it so certain that a married Poe might not actually have changed? Is it so certain that, at forty, he might not have reformed his old habits and settled in as a respected citizen of Richmond, with the *Stylus* taking a place at the head of American letters?

The picture of Poe, no longer vexed by life or by his own failings, growing contentedly into old age beside the girl he'd loved in his youth, must remain as a haunting possibility.

Appendix

The Letters of Elmira Shelton

No more than a half-dozen of Elmira Shelton's letters are known to have survived. Of the six, three are short notes of no great import (to John Ingram, George, Eveleth, and Edward Valentine, see the Notes). A fourth is quoted from at some length in my text (p. 25). The two others, both of fair length, are also quoted from in the text, but briefly, a telling phrase here and there. One, written to Mrs. Clemm just after Poe's death, shows with what a shock the news came to her, and how deeply she felt his loss, and for those reasons should be put fully on the record. The other is a rambling, offhand bit of casual correspondence, written almost a year before Poe came back into her life. It is valuable as showing, at least hinting at, a rather warm and attractive personality, one of strong religious cast. It also shows her—aged thirty-nine, and widowed for five years—as being in just the proper frame of mind for a new adventure of the heart. Such a susceptible mood, at such an age, faced with the sudden reawakening of an old, lamented love, is quite enough to explain Elmira's ready and rapid response to a man she hadn't met or been in touch with for fifteen years.

1.

Sarah Elmira Shelton to Mrs. Clemm, October 11, 1849. The original is lost, but it was published from manuscript in the *Century Magazine* in 1903, in "The Poe-Chivers Papers," edited by G. E. Woodberry. The printed version omits paragraphing, added here for clarity.

Richmond, Oct. 11th, 1849

Oh! how shall I address you, my dear, and deeply afflicted friend under such heart-rending circumstances! I have no doubt, ere this, you have heard of the death of *our dear Edgar!* yes, he was the *dearest object* on earth to me; and, well assured am I, that he was the pride of your heart.

I have not been able to get any of the particulars of his sickness & death, except an abstract from the *Baltimore Sun,* which said that he died on Sunday, the 7th of this month, with congestion of the brain, after an illness of 7 days.

He came up to my house on the evening of the 26th Sept. to take leave of me. He was very sad, and complained of being quite sick. I felt his pulse and found he had considerable fever, and did not think it probable he would be able to start the next morning (Thursday) as he anticipated. I felt so wretched about him all of that night, that I went up early next morning to enquire after him, when, much to my regret, he had left in the boat for Baltimore.

He expected certainly to have been with his "dear Muddy" on the Sunday following, when he promised to write to me; and after the expiration of a week, and no letter,

I became very uneasy, and continued in an agonizing state of mind, fearing he was ill, but never dreamed of his death, until it met my eye in glancing casually over a Richmond paper of last Tuesday.

Oh! my dearest friend! I cannot begin to tell you what my feelings were, as the horrible truth forced itself upon me! It was the most severe trial I have ever had; and God alone knows how I can bear it! My heart is overwhelmed—yes, ready to burst!

How can I, dear Muddy! speak comfort to your bleeding heart? I cannot say to you weep not—mourn not—but I do say, *do both,* for he is worthy to be lamented. Oh! my dear Edgar! shall I never behold your dear face and hear your sweet voice saying, "Dearest Muddy!" and "Dearest Elmira?"—how can I bear the separation?

The pleasure I had anticipated on his return with you, dear friend! to Richmond, was too great ever to be realized, and should teach me the folly of expecting bliss on earth. If it will be any consolation to you, my dear friend! to know that there is *one* who feels for you all that human can feel, then be assured that person is *Elmira.*

Willingly would I fly to you, if I could add to your comfort, or take from your sorrows. I wrote you a few weeks ago; I hope you received the letter. It was through the request of my dearest Eddy that I did so; and when I told him I had written to you, his joy & delight were inexpressible.

I hope you will write to me as soon as possible, and let me hear from you, as I shall be anxious about you incessantly until I do. Farewell, my stricken Friend! and may an All-Wise & Merciful God sustain and comfort us under this heart-breaking dispensation, is the fervent & hourly prayer of your Afflicted and sympathizing friend.

Elmira Shelton

Do let me hear from you as quickly as possible—Direct to Mrs. Elmira Shelton—Care of A. L. Royster, Richmond, Va.*

2.

Sarah Elmira Shelton to her cousin Philip Fitzhugh, December 11, 1848, written from Miller's Landing, Essex Co., Va. (the home of her widowed mother's family). From the original at the University of Texas. Not enough is known of her to explain her downhearted mention of "past events." It was only some seven months later that Poe came back into her life. The handwriting is small and graceful, a controlled hand well used to letter-writing. The engaging woman who wrote this pleasant if frank letter is not at all reflected in the two unfortunately tight-lipped photographs that survive of her. Why did it take early photographers so long to discover the magic of a smile?

December 11th 1848

My Dear Cousin

Having retired to my room this beautiful morning, I feel particularly in the humour for writing a meditation, and I feel at the same time that there is no one in this wide world who would be more pleased to receive a few lines from me, than my cousin Phil. Am I right in thus thinking? Or do I place myself too high in your affections?—I have been intending to write to you ever since I left home, but being always in company since my arrival here, and having two or

---

*This is her brother Alexander, aged thirty-three, whose house at Grace and 27th, southwest corner, stood one block from Elmira's own residence (*Montague's Richmond Directory,* p. 108). With Alexander lived his wife Susan, and their three young children, a girl and two boys (Census of 1850).

three letters to write every week to my relations in Richmond, must plead for me.

My health is very good, and the kindness & affection of my friends here, has I think improved and brightened up my drooping spirits, and which were in a very low and distressing condition when I left home, as you know. There is nothing (to me) more soothing than this pleasant mode of interchanging thoughts and feelings with those we love, and praised be the man who first invented letter writing.

Well how are [you] getting along my boy, in the way of Physic, love matters etc., first rate I expect. I received a letter from my dear Bettie a few days since, in which she informed me that you were appointed to deliver a lecture (in the spring) in behalf of the graduating class. I am delighted, tho' not at all surprised to hear it, and have no doubt of your acquitting yourself with much honour, and I do assure you, there is no one who will take more pleasure & delight in being present at that event, than your humble cousin E.

I have not had it in my power to visit Middlesex as I certainly anticipated, having had no opportunity of doing so. I do not think I shall now be able to do so, as I am getting a little home sick, and when I start, it must be towards Richmond. Bettie wrote me that she expected to start for King William last Saturday, and from thence to cousin Pat's to spend a week or two, but I think it very doubtful, whether she did or not.

Have you seen anyone who cares for, or inquires after me? I am inclined to think that my absence to *some few,* is much more desirable than my presence, but be that as it may, I delight and glory in a conscience void of offense towards my fellow creatures, and it is that which helps to buoy me up, and gives me resolution to hold a high head. If you should see my Cousin Charles, tell him I have not forgotten him, nor *ever shall,* and tell him I think he might drop me a friendly line now & then. I hope sincerely that he is getting along *bravely* & *happily.* Give him from me a devoted Cousin's love, and ask him if he wants to see me. There is no one I would be more pleased to see, than my cousins Charles and Philip. My heart is with you all, tho' I think it very doubtful whether I shall return until the 1st Jan'y.

I am fearful Cousin Philip, that I shall never be a happy woman again, time will certainly do a great deal in obliterating past events from my feelings, but I am certain that I shall never feel like myself again—I am conscious that I have erred (we all err) but mine have been truly errors of the *head,* not of the *heart*—I believe you Philip to be my friend, else I would not speak so candidly, or make thus free with you.

This is a world of troubles & disappointments, (at least I have found it so) tho' it is but a short journey to eternity, therefore it behooves me to be up and doing. I often ask myself can this heart which seems so full of corruption be a dwelling place for the "Holy Spirit?" Will he live where there are so many unholy thoughts and desires? Sanctify us Lord, and make each and every one of us who profess Thy Holy Name, meet for the inheritance of the Saints in Light.

I shall expect a letter from you by Friday's Mail. I must now bid you "Good bye" dear Cousin. Think of all that is meant by that expressive phrase:—and Oh! may Angels guard you, and may you be blessed forever. Thus prays your friend & Cousin

Elmira

Don't let the family see this letter, you know why— Can't you send me a few lines to write in a young lady's album? Direct your letters to Millers Essex—Care Capt. R. L. Covington.

Notes and Sources

This book's primary field of interest being so concentrated, some leeway in the matter of secondary references is allowable. I see little need for readers to wade through added bulky pages of citations extraneous to the main concern. For the generally accepted facts of Poe's life and his movements in the period under discussion—July–October 1849, including his final departure from Richmond, when the mystery proper begins—I have used the standard sources. This includes all the serious biographies from Ingram (1880) to Silverman (1991), and specialized studies and periodical literature where relevant. These books and articles I cite when emphasizing or adding to some received fact, but not otherwise, not when calling up scenes and incidents more or less familiar.

Readers who have a particular or professional interest in Poe matters will need no more than that. Other, more casual readers will have no wish for more.

Of course, everything else—especially everything on and after the crucial day of Poe's departure from Richmond, September 27, 1849—having the least connection with the mystery and its solution, is fully attended to in the Notes. For quoted matter the first few words of the quotation are repeated, enough to make identification sure. Sources, given here in shortened form, may be fully identified by a glance at the bibliography.

The left-hand margin displays *page* numbers.

Prologue: The Case Reopened

xi   *Poe's originality:* It is no longer necessary, I take it, to demonstrate that Poe was in fact the founder of mystery and detective fiction. A very few separate elements of the genre may have existed before him. But only in his stories were all the elements present, crystallized into a definite, recognizable, repeatable technique or formula, centering on the figure of the detective.

xii   *Suggested causes of Poe's death:* For the heart condition see the Allen biography, for the epilepsy see Fairfield, for the diabetic coma see Hill, for the meningitis see Robertson, for the hypoglycemia see Groves, for the toxic disorder see Bramsback, for the brain hemorrhage see Courtney, for the rabies see Benitez. (The election violence is detailed in Chapter Five.)

Such speculations are legitimate as far as they go, but none of those offered so far carry the stamp of conviction. The Benitez theory about rabies, for instance, reveals a somewhat shaky knowledge of Poe biography, and includes a medical diagnosis purely fanciful ("No evidence of trauma . . . the pulse rate was in the 50s and 'thready' . . . neurologic examination showed the patient was alert . . . there was no tremor," etc.). Rabies requires an animal bite, of course, and Benitez admits there is no record of Poe's having been bitten. But rabies "may have a long incubation period," he adds, and on that convenient basis concludes that Poe's supposed encounter with a rabid animal was "distant and forgotten."

xiii "Long-continued intoxication"—Griswold, *Miscellany,* 338–39.

xiii "A day of wild debauchery"—Daniel, 178.

xiii "no reliable evidence"—Silverman, 433.

xiii "The precise circumstances"—Carlson, 23.

One: Enter Poe

1 *The American Hotel:* Phillips, 1452, gives a contemporary illustration, also showing Main Street, part of the downtown, and one of the city's omnibuses. See also Weiss, 708, and Thomas, *Log,* 818.

2 *Poe's Philadelphia binge:* The standard portrayal of this episode may be followed in Woodberry, II, 309–13, Allen, 649–51, Quinn, 614–19, Silverman, 414–19. Also the sources for Sartain and Lippard in Chapter Six.

3 "Think of the blow"—*Letters,* II, 454. It seems he recovered only one of the two lost lectures, for the three times he spoke on this trip, twice in Richmond and once in Norfolk, were all on the same topic, *The Poetic Principle.* Rather than the lectures having been stolen, as he feared, it is likely that he simply left one of them behind in New York.

4 "My clothes are so"—*Letters,* II, 454. He doesn't say what was wrong with his clothes that made them horrible. After his Philadelphia spree they were probably

at least wrinkled and dust-covered. But more than the condition of his clothes, it was his suddenly despondent mood that dictated his reaction. The "awfully hot" weather he mentions in a letter written to Mrs. Clemm on July 14th, the day he arrived by steamboat in Richmond (*Letters,* II, 453).

Two: Enter the Widow

5   *The Shelton house:* Phillips, 1435, gives a later photograph. Still standing, it is still a private dwelling.

5   *Mrs. Shelton's background:* All that is known of Elmira Shelton occurs in connection with Poe, and is available in the standard biographies. Rather strangely, she has never been made the object of much individual study. The only separate articles are the ones by Dietz, which gives little about her personally but much about her descendants, and Rein, which discusses the love affair, both in youth and later. She is also mentioned at more or less length in many other articles, notably those by Weiss, Alfriend, Woodberry (1903), and Ingram (1878). Also see Mabbott, *Wilmer's Merlin,* and Allen and Mabbott, *Poe's Brother.*

Elmira's daughter, Ann, and her son, Southall, are always described as "schoolchildren" (Mabbott, *Annals,* 567), their ages given as about the same, twelve and ten. But Ann's age is given as nineteen in the U.S. Census of 1850, and her birthday is listed in Moore, *Henrico,* 280, as February 6, 1830. Her correct age is important since it shows that her opposition to her mother's marrying Poe was not the petulant rejection of a child. Within a year or two of Poe's death, Ann married John

Leftwich of Richmond, and bore four children. Southall eventually married and fathered two children. By 1950, Elmira's direct descendants numbered at least thirty (Dietz, 38, 44). Ann's daughter Jennie, who lived for many years with her grandmother, did not know of the Poe connection until her own maturity: "No mention of Poe was ever made in her family" while Elmira lived (Dietz, 41). This accords with what is stated in my Epilogue.

6 "lovely, almost saintly"—Alfriend, 490. My description of Elmira is also from Alfriend, a Richmond man who knew her in her last years, and whose father knew her in youth. Many others who knew her agreed that as a young girl she had been compellingly attractive, mentioning the blue eyes and the sweet voice.

7 *Elmira and Poe in youth:* Her father's fatal interference, said Elmira in the Valentine interview, was prompted only by her age, then 15, and that may be. But it is also suggested that Mr. Royster acted as he did only after being told that Poe would not be the heir of his wealthy foster-father, John Allen (see Dietz, 39). The two families did live near each other in Richmond, and the two fathers knew each other well. The added details of the youthful affair in Phillips and Allen are pure hearsay, of late date and at third or fourth hand.

8 "I shall never forget"— Quinn and Hart, 27, which prints the full letter. This confession of Elmira, to my mind, is quite enough to establish the full reality of the early love between her and Poe. The incident she reports occurred some eight years after her marriage, when she had already borne, and lost, one child. Here she writes about the incident after still another dozen

years. A fuller description of the encounter, supposedly supplied to J. H. Whitty by Elmira herself (perhaps through a third party) shows her entering a large hall where a gala reception is under way. She removes her cloak and hands it to an attendant, when

> suddenly she glanced down toward the crowded end of the reception room, and there she met the gaze of two dark eyes. Poe never for a single moment relaxed his gaze. Elmira afterwards stated that she could not for the life of her do aught but return his gaze— becoming riveted to the spot. Their old love affair was well understood by many of those present; and Elmira only realized the dramatic situation in which she stood when her husband approached and hurried her to the dressing room, secured her wrap, hurried her into a carriage, and drove home, where there was another scene. (Quoted in Phillips, 276; no specific citation given beyond Whitty, who contributed a foreword to the Phillips volume.)

Another strong indication of the true depth and reality of this youthful love is the fact that its breakup sparked two long compositions besides Poe's own *Tamerlane.* One was by Poe's brother (*The Pirate,* a prose tale published in the Baltimore *North American* in 1827), and one by Poe's friend Lambert Wilmer (*Merlin,* a three-act play published in the *North American,* also in 1827). None of these compositions, including Poe's, is memorable. But an incident of the heart which could have inspired three such lengthy compositions could hardly have been trivial. Missing from the record is Elmira's own girlhood reaction to this minor literary hubbub over her doomed romance. Certainly it was one of the things that kept the memory of her youthful love so alive in her heart.

9 *Elmira's last sight of Poe before 1849:* Some biographers accept a meeting between the two during Poe's 1848 visit to Richmond (for instance, Silverman, 852), where others deny it (for instance, Quinn, 629). But the evidence, such as it is, really affords no firm basis at all for such a meeting. It depends wholly on Mrs. Whitman's memory of what Poe supposedly told her, recorded in a letter of Mrs. Whitman's written twenty years later. Nothing in the sparse record left by Elmira herself, or in any other record, lends the least weight to the claim of a meeting in 1848, or at any other time back to the year 1836. Poe may well have talked to Mrs. Whitman in the fall of 1848 about Mrs. Shelton, but it is clear that she later put her own twist on whatever he said.

9 "that I shall never"—From the original letter at the University of Texas. For the full text see the Appendix.

10 *Susan Talley (later Mrs. Weiss):* Her only unusual recognition as a poet came with her appearance in Griswold's *Female Poets of America* of 1848 (along with no less than ninety-two others, rather diluting the honor!). Four of her poems are given, showing little more than glibness and a knack for imitation. A biographical sketch in the same volume notes that at age nine she "entirely lost her hearing." She also painted, it is said, her work being "praised by the best critics in the arts of design." But neither as poet nor painter did she make any sort of mark.

11 "a mysterious being"—Weiss, 708–09. She adds that reading his stories in youth, especially *King Pest,* "every word of which I received as truth," left her haunted by feelings of "unspeakable horror," no doubt in a

deliciously shivery way. It is evident that coming face to face with the author of that horror, though she was then somewhat older, left her a bit shaken as well as captivated.

11   "I regarded the meeting"—Weiss, 708. Same for the quotations in the next five paragraphs describing this meeting.

13   "a gentleman in the"—From the original manuscript of the Valentine interview with Mrs. Shelton, November 19, 1875, in the Poe collection of the Valentine Museum, Richmond. The interview was first published in part in *Appleton's Journal,* May 1878, and has since been much quoted from. Same for the other quotations in this and the next paragraph.

15   *Elmira's sending word to Poe:* That Mrs. Shelton managed to get a quiet word to Poe about her possible interest in a renewal of their old romance, through the MacKenzie family, is stated or implied in a number of sources. See Weiss, 710, Weiss, *Home,* 196, and Harrison, *Century,* 451.

15   "When he did call"—Valentine interview, original ms. p. 5.

16   *The first Richmond lecture:* Within a year of Poe's death the lecture was published (*Home Journal,* August 31, 1850), which I think would not have pleased him, the talk having been designed for platform delivery where the effect sought was different from print. His use of the Willis poem—hardly more than a versified editorial—for that time and place was more than a little daring, and for him surprising.

16   "In a graceful attitude"—Thomas, *Log,* 825, quoting J. E. Cooke, who attended the lecture. For other firsthand references to the lecture see Thomas, *Log,* 826–28.

19   "arose, but made no"—Weiss, *Home,* 200. Same for the
next quotation in this paragraph.

Added Note to Chapter Two

A supposed pencil-sketch of Elmira as a teenager,
long claimed to be by Poe himself (original at the Lilly
Library, Indiana University), is almost certainly spurious. It appeared first in 1922, was privately rejected as
a fake, then surfaced again in 1930, when it was purchased by J. K. Lilly Jr., who was unaware of the earlier
incident. Two other drawings were included in the sale,
again supposedly by Poe, a self-portrait, and a picture
of his wife Virginia (See *New York Times,* September 22,
and October 4, 1930; *The Indiana Bookman,* March
1960; David Randall, *The J. K. Lilly Collection of EAP:
An Account of Its Formation,* 1964, 15–21). Though the
provenance of the sketches was known to be tainted,
up through the sixties they were at times included in
serious Poe biographical works. The self-portrait, looking more like Hawthorne than Poe, can be seen in *Letters,* II, 213.

The unknown forger based his efforts on good information. Both Poe and Elmira make direct reference to
his habit of throwing off sketches of her in their youthful days, references which were available in print well
before the turn of the century. In *Appleton's* in 1878 she
is quoted as saying that "Poe drew beautifully, and drew
a pencil likeness of me in a few minutes" (see under
Ingram, who quotes from the Valentine interview, the
line more correctly reading "drew a likeness of me with
a pencil in a very few minutes"). Poe in a letter to Mrs.
Clemm of September 1849 refers to "one of the pencil-

sketches of her [Elmira] that I took a long while ago in Richmond" (*Letters,* II, 459). This letter, including this remark, was published in the *Century* in 1894 (see under Woodberry), also in the Woodberry biography of 1909, p. 328. With two such definite sources to rely on for confirmation, any professional forger of historic art would have felt quite safe, and the first rebuff in 1922 must have taken him by surprise.

Hervey Allen in 1926 described a sketch portrait of Elmira "by Poe's own hand" (p. 119), which he saw in the possession of a Richmond collector, C. H. Barney. This picture *may* be authentic, for it was *not* the Lilly specimen. Allen describes the girl's hair as "a tangle of pretty curls," where the spurious drawing shows a page-boy bob. The present location of the Barney sketch I have not been able to trace.

Three: "We Regret to Learn . . ."

21   *Poe's temperance pledge:* Reported in many sources: see two notes down. I think there can be no question that, had it not been for Elmira, Poe would never in his life have taken such a step, wholly out of character for him.

22   "a dress coat"—*Letters,* II, 459. Same for his mention of the wedding ring, and for the next quotation in this paragraph. Several sources claim that the engagement was reported in the newspapers, but so far as I can find there were no printed references to the event. Of course, that would not have prevented the news from spreading rather quickly through Richmond society.

22   "It will be gratifying"—Moore, "Note," 360. This article first established the date of the pledge. Poe sent his signed pledge card on to Mrs. Clemm, who sent it in a

letter of her own to Annie Richmond. "The dark dark clouds I think are beginning to break," she wrote, "God of his great mercy grant he may keep this pledge" (Letter of September 15, 1849, University of Virginia). The pledge was administered by William Glenn, presiding officer of the Shockoe Hill Division. In a letter of June 1899 Glenn adds that his organization found no sign that Poe, up to his leaving the city, had violated his pledge. "In discussing the matter after his death," wrote Glenn, "the consensus of opinion of the temperance men was that he had kept his pledge inviolate up to that time" (From the original letter at the Valentine Museum, Richmond). Glenn and his colleagues had such a strong interest in the matter of Poe's fate — whether it had in fact resulted from drinking — that they later made inquiries in Baltimore, supposedly getting from Dr. Moran his assurance that Poe had not been drunk, "but was under the influence of a drug" (Letter of Glenn quoted in Harrison, 321). That claim, however, was made as late as 1900, and its distortion of whatever Moran told the inquirer represents only wishful thinking. None of the Richmond Sons of Temperance cared to have it said that a famous writer, six weeks after joining them, died of a debauch.

22 *The two drinking episodes in Richmond:* Weiss, 709, 712, and Carter, 566. They could not have been very blatant or public, for there exist no reverberations of them in other sources. That observation has special relevance for the second of the two supposed episodes, which Mrs. Weiss paints as so serious that "during some days his life was in imminent danger," leading his doctors to warn that a repeat performance "would prove fatal" (712). But Weiss admits that *at the time,* while she'd

"heard something," it was only "long afterward" that she understood about the drinking. Curiously uncritical has been the biographical use of Mrs. Weiss' memory as to Poe's besetting habit. Silverman, as did all before him, accepts her claim without question, mistakenly adding as if on her authority that "The doctors diagnosed his condition as 'mania a potu' . . ." (427). But Weiss nowhere employs the term *mania a potu,* gives no sign of actual delirium being in question. My own conclusion is that she has confused a known incident of the prior year, 1848, when Poe was also briefly in Richmond, and drinking heavily (see any of the biographies), with a couple of much slighter indulgences of his 1849 visit.

23   "no great rapture"— Quinn, 629.

23   *Elmira's inheritance:* Thomas, *Log,* 839, which quotes from the original will of Alexander Shelton on file in the Henrico County Courthouse. Prior to discovery of this will, Poe biographers all assumed, quite wrongly, that Elmira herself had made arrangements to put her fortune legally beyond Poe's reach when he became her husband.

24   "He was the *dearest*"—Woodberry, *Century,* 551, which quotes the entire letter. The original was among the papers of T. H. Chivers, who received it from Mrs. Clemm when he was thinking of writing a Poe biography. See Appendix for the complete letter.

24   "I think she loves"—*Letters,* II, 461. Some phrases in another letter of Poe's written now seem to reveal him a good deal colder. From Old Point Comfort, where he'd gone to lecture, he wrote Mrs. Clemm about the impending wedding, saying that immediately afterward they would all go to "one of her houses—the one she is

in now." Then he advises Mrs. Clemm to be ready but not to sell anything yet, "for 'there is many a slip between the cup and the lip,' and I confess that my heart sinks at the idea of this marriage. I think, however, that it will certainly take place, and that immediately" (Letter of September 10, 1849, from the original at Fales Library, New York University). But a possible slip between cup and lip, and his heart sinking "at the idea of this marriage," I believe are entirely referable to the opposition being mounted to the marriage by Elmira's children and relatives. He worries not only that they may succeed in halting it, he also shrinks from the threat of trouble in the future, after the marriage has taken place. See Chapter Three for discussion of the negative attitude taken by the children and relatives. Another of his remarks at this time, about Annie Richmond, his Lowell friend, is not so revealing as it may seem. Talking about where he and Elmira will make their home, he adds, "I *must* be somewhere I can see Annie" (Letter to Mrs. Clemm, II, 454). Of course this is the famous author speaking, not the man. Annie was simply the ardent acolyte Poe as a writer needed and craved, a source of unquestioning devotion possessing an elegant home in which he was always welcome.

25 "My Dear Mrs. Clemm"—Quinn and Hart, 26–27. She adds that Edgar spoke affectionately of his dead wife, "for which I but love him the more."

25 *The wedding date:* First revealed as October 17th by J. H. Whitty in his "Memoir" (1911), the information coming, he said, from old Richmond informants. Whitty, who had been engaged in Poe research from about 1875, did enjoy many contacts among Richmond people who had known Poe.

26   *The Loud commission: Letters,* II, 458, 727. Poe had included Mrs. Loud in his *Autography* article (*Graham's,*
December 1841), and she also made an appearance in
Griswold's *Female Poets of America* (again, as one of
ninety-two entries, half of whom didn't merit inclusion). She gets only a one-paragraph introduction but
has the benefit of a favorable quote from Poe's *Autography* piece.

27   "would mimic the"—Dietz, 40. Same for the other two
quotations in the paragraph.

27   *Objection by Elmira's relatives:* This is stated explicitly
by Mrs. Weiss (Susan Talley), who quotes a Richmond
resident—Miss Van Lew, one-time city postmistress
and a next-door neighbor of the Sheltons—as saying
to her in conversation, "all her relatives are said to
be opposed to the match" (Weiss, *Home,* 196). I have
found no other overt source for the claim but several
biographers assume it. In any case, those relatives, hearing the stories about the poet that filtered down from
the north, would naturally have had good cause for
alarm. The Colton remark is in *Passages from the Correspondence of Rufus Griswold,* ed. W. Griswold (Cambridge, 1898), 262.

28   *Poe's affairs with women:* The facts about Poe and Mrs.
Whitman, Mrs. Osgood, and Mrs. Ellet, plus his more
minor links with such as Mrs. Shew and Mrs. Lewis,
are all readily available in the standard biographies.
The bastardy charge with regard to Fanny Osgood is
detailed in my own prior volume, *Plumes,* where the
related Ellet affair is also covered in some original detail. About little Fanny Fay, the essential point is not
whether she was in fact Poe's child, but that many in-
siders would have concluded that she *was.*

      That all this gossip about Poe's female entanglements, both real and exaggerated, did in fact reach the ears of many in Richmond, there is hardly a need to discuss. Between New York, New England, and Richmond, especially in journalistic circles, there was a steady flow back and forth of news, rumor, and gossip. One definite channel existed between John Daniel, editor of the Richmond *Examiner,* and Mrs. Whitman, the two being well acquainted. Mrs. Whitman's own short-lived engagement to Poe affords a convincing and rather startling parallel. As is well known, she was repeatedly warned by mail, some of it anonymous, against Poe's supposed moral delinquencies and character flaws, predicting only tragedy if she married him. (See for instance Ticknor, 118–134, and any of the standard biographies.) Those same ill-disposed informants would not have hesitated to raise a similar alarm in Elmira's case, working mostly through her many Richmond relatives.

In fact, Poe was dead only a matter or weeks when all the ugly tales about him, accurate or not, began to find their way into print, starting with the Whitman engagement. The Griswold "Memoir" in the *International Miscellany,* March 1850, states that "the breaking of the engagement affords a striking illustration of his character," then proceeds to describe him in Providence, where Mrs. Whitman lived, as "reeling through the streets of the city." He invaded Mrs. Whitman's home, wrote Griswold, as if on good authority, where "in his drunkenness he committed . . . such outrages as made necessary a summons of the police. Here was no insanity leading to indulgence: he went from New York with a determination thus to induce an ending of the engagement; and he succeeded." Such stories, this one and worse, were whispered about and guessed at

even while he was smilingly welcomed into Richmond homes during that last visit of his life in July–
September 1849.

31   "received with rounds"—Thomas, *Log,* 836, quoting
the Norfolk paper, *American Beacon.* Same for the other
quotations concerning the Norfolk lecture.

31   *The appointment with Mrs. Loud:* Dates for this were discussed in a letter of Poe to Mrs. Loud, September 18,
1849 (*Letters,* II, 726). He says he'll be in Philadelphia
on the 26th, and asks if that will suit. If she wrote back
to delay the meeting to the 27th, that would account
for Poe waiting until that morning to depart. The book
of poetry he was to have "edited" for Mrs. Loud appeared in the fall of 1850, without Poe's help.

31   *Poe's movements in Richmond, September 25–26:* Carter,
565–66, Whitty, "Memoir," lxxxiii, Weiss, 714, and
Weiss, *Home,* 203–04 (the Weiss inaccuracies in detail
do not vitiate the general picture she provides).

31   "Here's a little trifle"—Allen, 668.

33   "very sad"—Elmira to Mrs. Clemm, Woodberry, *Century,* 551. Same for the other quotation in this paragraph and the next. Elmira does not say explicitly that
she went to the Swan tavern that morning (she wrote,
"I went up early next morning to enquire after him"),
but since he was then staying at the Swan, it is evident
she would have gone there.

34   *Elmira's finding of the death notice:* The moment is briefly
described in her letter to Mrs. Clemm, quoted in Woodberry, *Century,* 552. She says that when she didn't hear
from Poe she began to fear that he'd fallen ill along the
way, "but never dreamed of his death, until it met my
eye in glancing casually over a Richmond paper of last
Tuesday."

34   "I cannot begin to"—Woodberry, *Century,* 552.

35   "obscured and crippled"—Thomas, *Log,* 852.

35   *Poe's burial:* There has always been disagreement as to
       how many were present that day and who they were. A
       total of ten—four in addition to the mourners—does
       seem correct, as follows: Rev. William Clemm, who
       read the service, Neilson Poe, Dr. Snodgrass, Henry
       Herring, Mrs. Elizabeth Herring Smith and her hus-
       band, Joseph Clarke, Poe's old schoolmaster, Z. C. Lee,
       a boyhood friend, sexton George Spencer, and under-
       taker Charles Suter. It was the quick burial, less than
       twenty-four hours after death, that prevented many
       more people from hearing the news and attending the
       funeral. Why burial couldn't have been held up a day or
       two, and who made the decision to go ahead, are unan-
       swerable questions. Years later the Rev. Clemm recalled
       that it was Neilson Poe who told him of Poe's death and
       invited him to officiate at the burial (Bramsback, 55,
       quoting Clemm's letter of 1889, at the University of
       Virginia. See also Quinn and Hart, 30).

Four: Witness Time

36   "arrived in this city"—New York *Herald,* October 9,
       1849. Preceding the Poe item in the column are the
       details of a Baltimore Fair and Cattle Show.

37   *Gunner's Hall:* This building, located at 44 Lombard
       Street, between High and Exeter, is specified in the Bal-
       timore *Sun* (3 October 1849) as the general site of the
       Fourth Ward polls, which were in the hall "at Ryan's
       Tavern."

39   "At what time he arrived"—Quinn and Hart, 30.

40   "Records of the case"—Quinn and Hart, 33. Same for
       the other quotations in this paragraph.

41   "Presuming you are"—Quinn and Hart, 32.

42   "At this he broke"—Quinn and Hart, 33.

43   "wore an aspect of"—Snodgrass, *Life,* 24. It must have been Snodgrass himself who alerted Herring.

43   "His hat—or rather the"—Snodgrass, *Life,* 24. Same for the quotations in the next two paragraphs.

45   "head dropped forward"—Snodgrass, *Beadle's,* 283. The description of his clothing closely echoes the earlier list he gave in the *Life* article: "a rusty, almost brimless, tattered and ribbonless palm-leaf hat. His clothing consisted of a sack-coat of thin and sleazy black alpaca, ripped more or less at several of its seams, and faded and soiled, and pants of a steel-mixed pattern of cassinette [cassimere] half-worn and badly fitting, if they could be said to fit at all. He wore neither vest nor neck-cloth, while the bosom of his shirt was both crumpled and badly soiled." Then follows the mention of the boots as given in the text. This *Beadle's* article by Snodgrass was actually prompted, as he admits, by an earlier *Beadle's* piece that same year, authored by Mrs. E. O. Smith (February 1867).

     Several writers reject the description of Poe at Ryan's as given by Snodgrass in his *Beadle's* article. The charge is that he "disgracefully misquoted" Walker's note, making much uglier Poe's physical condition: "Whereas Walker spoke of a 'gentleman rather the worse for wear,' Snodgrass substituted 'in a state of beastly intoxication.'" (Bandy, "Myth," 27; see also Spencer, *Herald,* 1881). An ardent temperance man, Snodgrass is accused of deliberately darkening the portrait for his own crusading purposes. But of course this misses the whole point (and overlooks Snodgrass' earlier *Life* description). In paraphrasing Walker's note, Snodgrass is silently adding what he *saw* with his own eyes that day at

Ryan's. He is not offering Walker as his authority, he is giving in detail what he himself *witnessed.* Another phrase in the Walker note, seldom noticed, fully supports Snodgrass: Poe at Ryan's was "in great distress."

46 *The Walker note:* Snodgrass' widow allowed the note to be copied for W. H. Browne of the *Southern Magazine,* and to be quoted with other Poe letters in the *Herald* article by Spencer of March 1881 (Miller, *Building,* 85). The original note is lost. Walker's having worked for Snodgrass explains how he knew where to send the note: Snodgrass then lived at 103 High Street, some two blocks north of Ryan's place (Gunner's Hall was destroyed by fire in 1904). The absence of Walker's own testimony from the record is unfortunate—again, something an inquest would have avoided. By the time anyone went looking for Walker—in 1880, after the finding of his note—he was dead (Miller, *Building,* 86).

After dispatching his note to Snodgrass, no doubt by messenger, Walker didn't remain on the premises but left, as he says, "in haste." Whether Snodgrass later sought him out to gain more information is unknown. Probably not, for then we would have the answer to another nagging question: did Walker find Poe already seated in the bar, or did he find him outside and kindly help him in? My own solution, in Chapter Eight, concludes that he found him already inside. Probably, Walker went to Ryan's that day in order to cast his vote in the election. *Why* he stopped to speak with an inebriated patron is more information lost because there was no police inquiry.

Voter traffic at Ryan's Tavern on election day was heavy, so that the inebriated Poe slumped in a chair would have drawn little attention. Returns in the congressional race, Fourth Ward, counting both Demo-cratic and Whig tickets, totaled 903 (Baltimore *Sun,* 4 October 1849). That puts the hourly rate of arrivals at about one hundred, meaning that the tavern was crowded all day long, perhaps heaviest in late afternoon when Poe was found. Just why Joseph Walker in these busy circumstances stopped to talk with the distressed Poe becomes even more a matter of curiosity. His note to Snodgrass offers no clue.

47   "He succumbed to"—New York *Herald,* October 28, 1875. Same for the quotations in the next paragraph.

48   *Conductor Rollins:* Nothing is known of the train con-ductor beyond what is given by Moran. Baltimore City directories for 1847–54 supply one George Rollin [no s], but he was a steamboat agent. There are also a Capt. William Rollins of the ship *Isabel,* and five other Rollinses, none of them train conductors. Note that the earliest reference, very brief, to Poe on the train being turned back at Havre de Grace occurs in Stoddard's *Harper's* piece of 1872 ("he was brought back from Havre de Grace by the conductor of the Philadelphia train, in a state of delirium . . ."). From other stray bits of information in this article it is certain that Stoddard was in direct touch with Dr. Moran.

48   "When he reached the"—Moran, *Defense,* 58–59. Mo-ran's little book—eighty-five pages and paperbound—has not fared well among Poe scholars, and with reason. His many errors and distortions (a result of carelessness and a wish to please) and his foolish attempt to make the dying poet sound properly mystical, are enough to condemn his work generally. Yet he does have a few valuable things to offer. He was in touch with Elmira Shelton, and for many years maintained an interest in

Poe. An example of how he tends to be ignored (again, in good part his own fault), is found in *The Poe Log* (Thomas and Jackson). Quoted at length in the *Log's* text is Moran's important letter to Mrs. Clemm of November 9th describing Poe's last hours. But in the *Log's* "Biographical Notes On Persons Mentioned In the Text" his name is missing.

49 "He who arched the"—Moran, *Defense,* 72. Same for the next quotation in this paragraph.

50 "At Havre de Grace"—Gill, 237. It is evident that Gill's source was the expected one, Dr. Moran, who had not then published anything on Poe. Gill's way of explaining Poe's death was simply to combine Moran, Spencer, and Stoddard. He has Poe brought back from Havre de Grace to Baltimore where he is captured by the election "coopers" and imprisoned: "He arrived at night. It was the eve of a municipal election . . . wandering through the streets he was seized by the ruffianly agents of one of the political clubs, and locked up for the night . . . the next day he was taken out, still in a state of delirium, and made to repeat votes at eleven different wards."

50 *Poe's trunk:* This intriguing item has been paid very little attention in Poe biography, resulting in some disagreement as to its fate. But there is really no need for confusion. In a letter of March 1850, Mrs. Clemm thanks Moran for his part in finding it: "In November last I received a letter from Neilson Poe, saying that you had placed in his possession my son's trunk, and asking me in what way he was to dispose of it. I instantly replied to him requesting him to send it on to me, that I alone had any claim to it." (Moran, *Defense,* 16). That the trunk was in fact sent to her is proved by a letter

written in December 1876 by the sister of Annie Richmond. She mentions having "an early edition of Mr. Poe's works," and adds, "It was found in the trunk which was forwarded to Mrs. Clemm from Baltimore soon after his death" (Miller, *Building,* 156; for further discussion see Quinn, 656–57; Woodberry, *Life,* 451).

Moran himself in later telling of his finding of the trunk again flew the track. He has an elaborate scene in the hospital in which a clearheaded Poe (!) replies to questions, in one of which he tells the doctor that his trunk was left at "a hotel on Pratt Street, opposite the depot." (*Defense,* 64; see also 16, 55). Moran says he promptly sent a porter over to the hotel, who brought back the trunk. Of course, this is more of Moran's inevitable posturing, but in it is a grain of truth. Moran did procure the trunk, but not until afterward, probably in November, and very probably, as he indicates, at Bradshaw's Hotel on Pratt Street.

Today at the Poe Foundation Shrine in Richmond there is a trunk exhibited as the original. It was sent there by an anonymous donor in 1929, ultimately deriving, it is said, from Poe's sister Rosalie. While its provenance is uncertain, physically it could indeed be the original. Made of black leather (now much faded) over wood, reinforced by metal strips, it is 18 inches high, 27 inches wide, and 17 inches deep. Though the actual trunk when found had first been sent to Mrs. Clemm in Lowell in 1850, it is possible that it later came into Rosalie's possession. During 1870 the two women lived in neighboring cities, Baltimore and Washington, in charity homes. Mrs. Clemm died in February 1871, upon which the trunk may have come to Rosalie, who lived to 1874.

Five: Five Lost Days

53 "the facts, as far as"—Stoddard, 568. An earlier article on Poe by Stoddard (*National Magazine,* March 1853) has no mention of the "cooping" claim. Not irrelevant in the present context, I think, is Stoddard's well-known hatred of Poe, expressed in a half-dozen articles over some forty years (see my *Plumes, passim*).

54 "the victim of the most"—Baird, 199. For the little that is known of Baird and his association with the *Southern Magazine,* see Miller, *Building,* 68–70.

54 "At that time, and for"—Quoted in Miller, *Building,* 69.

55 "The Reform Association"—Quoted in Miller, *Building,* 69. Same for the next quotation in this paragraph. Scharf himself (*not* his book) may have been the ultimate source or authority used by Thompson for his "cooping" idea. A late claim about an encounter with Poe in a Baltimore oyster-bar just before he was seized by the "coopers" is an obvious invention (Didier, *Cult,* 177–78).

56 *Stoddard and Thompson:* In his *Harper's* article, Stoddard gives details of Poe's 1849 visit to Richmond which clearly came from Thompson in conversation—the information he uses appeared only much later in print (1894) in the note by Dimmock in *Harper's* (which unfortunately confuses the visits of 1848 and 1849). That the two men in fact were close friends during Thompson's seven years as a New York editor is seen in his appointing Stoddard to be his literary executor (obituary, New York *Evening Post,* May 1, 1873).

57 "The manner of his death"—Thompson, *Genius,* 42.

57 "made to repeat votes"—Gill, 238.

58 "twaddle"—Mabbott, *Works*, II, 569.

58 "proceeded by boat"—Ingram, 426. For Ingram's contacts with Browne and others in Baltimore see Miller, *Building*, 65–67. Further interesting data on the point is in Miller, *Helen*.

59 "Since writing the other"—Miller, *Building*, 85.

60 "hunting up all about"—Miller, *Building*, 86.

61 "immediate proximity as"—Spencer, *Herald*. Same for all the following quotations from Spencer.

62 "Eight blocks east of"—Spencer, *Herald*, 27 March 1881.

63 "fanciful"—Carlson, 24.

64 "There was very little"—Baltimore *Sun*, 4 October 1849. Next day the *Sun* observed in the same vein: "*Dull Business*—During the last three or four days the police docket has indicated a dull business in that department of municipal affairs. The loafers, rowdies, and outsiders have certainly left the city, or else they have 'gone in their holes' for a season. It speaks well for a large city like Baltimore." In plainer words, no public violence of any sort had come to police attention.

65 "resting place"—Carter, 565.

66 "one evening about half"—Carter, 565. Aside from this article, the little that is known of Dr. Carter can be found in Woodberry, II, 322, 341, 430, and in Weiss, *Home*, 203–04. Poe's visit to the Carter office that last night in Richmond had actually been recorded, in passing, years earlier in Susan Talley's first article (1878) but little attention had been paid to the fact (Weiss, 714). In that same article, interestingly, she also mentions Poe's taking the cane from Carter's office, and not returning it. Her source, I assume, would have been Carter himself.

Six: The Sartain Interval

69   "on a hot summer day"—Eaves, 46. The entire Lippard article, an obscure one first published in 1853 in *The Sunday Mercury* (Philadelphia), is reprinted by Eaves. Same for the Lippard quotations in the next several paragraphs.

72   "The last time I saw"—Sartain, "Reminiscences," 413.

75   "These are examples"—Sartain, "Reminiscences," 414–15.

77   "The first instance of"—Sartain, "Last Days," in Tuerk, 22, which reprints the entire *Transcript* article.

78   "By and by I suggested"—Sartain, "Last Days," in Tuerk, 22.

79   "dread of some fearful"—Gill, 234. Gill says that he received the story from "an old-time associate of the poet," meaning Sartain. His dating of the incident is vaguely referred to Poe's "last visit to Philadelphia, which took place at this time," leaving uncertain what the phrase "this time" meant. Gill adds that when Poe burst in on Sartain he was "in a highly excited condition, almost distracted indeed. His mind seemed bewildered and oppressed." When the two went out for their walk to the Schuylkill, says Gill, Poe talked of "the fearful conspiracy which threatened his destruction." But, again, there's no word of suicide.

80   "The very instant you"—*Letters,* II, 452.

80   *Poe in Philadelphia in September–October 1849:* Briefly in both 1847 (August) and 1848 (fall) Poe passed through Philadelphia, but on neither of these visits was he drinking. Nor did he remain long in town, and there is no record of any sort of his suffering personal distress. Sartain in his several articles always referred his Poe

interlude to the fall of 1849, "a short time previous to his death" (Gill, 234), or "about a month before his tragic death" (*Transcript,* in Tuerk, 22). Added support for my claim that Poe in September–October reached Philadelphia before backtracking to Baltimore is supplied in Quinn, 637, but the evidence appears much too tenuous for stressing. It seems that an elderly relative of a college friend of Quinn's recalled that Poe, supposedly headed for New York, stayed overnight with still another relative, James Moss of South Fourth Street. Even if true, the visit cannot be pinpointed as to the year.

Concerning the Loud appointment, it can be said that Poe did *not* call on Mrs. Loud when he reached Philadelphia, a fact made clear by a notice in the *International Miscellany* (August 26, 1850) of her volume: "Mrs. M. St. Leon Loud, of Philadelphia, has in the press of Ticknor, Reed, and Fields, of Boston, a collection of her poems, entitled 'Wayside Flowers.' Mrs. Loud is a writer of much grace and elegance, and occasionally of a rich and delicate fancy. The late Mr. Poe was accustomed to praise her work very highly, and was to have edited this edition of them."

81 "looking pale and"—Sartain, "Reminiscences," 413. Same for the next two quotations in this paragraph.

83 *Date of the Lippard incident:* A brief, rather generalized article published four years after Poe's death, the Lippard piece offers only one internal clue as to dates. It was, he begins, "On a hot summer day, when the cholera was in the city." This does seem to indicate midsummer, July or August, for the disease in Philadelphia—and along the whole eastern seaboard—was then at its height. But the epidemic was very slow to clear off, and the weather continued hot into September. An error of some weeks in Lippard's memory, gener-

ated by confusion generally as to what happened when, would not be surprising, including a mistake as to the weather. In any case, Lippard's reason for writing the piece was not to chronicle Poe's movements. It was to roundly condemn the "literary hucksters," publishers and editors, who were so quick to heap praise on the dead poet after neglecting him in life.

There is also the implicit contradiction between Sartain and Lippard as to Poe's asking for pecuniary help. On leaving Sartain Poe borrowed a sum of money ("What was needful," *Lippincott's,* 415; "for his expenses." Philadelphia *Press*). But Lippard says that Poe came to him precisely because he was destitute and needed help to continue his journey ("I only want enough to get me out of Philadelphia. . . . For God's sake don't fail me!"). It is Poe's letter to Mrs. Clemm, written on his arrival in Richmond, which clinches a recent prior encounter with Lippard (if not a visit to his office). He says he is greatly indebted to several people for help in getting him out of Philadelphia: to Lippard, to Chauncey Burr, and "in some measure" to Sartain (*Letters,* II, 455; Burr was one of those who contributed). So the question may be asked, is it possible that Lippard in his article made the same fundamental gaffe as did Sartain, weaving together two encounters close in time? Did Poe perhaps descend on Lippard in *both* July and September, as he did on Sartain? Improbable as that seems, I would not like to rule it out. In fact one curious paragraph in his article appears to lend support to the idea. Poe, says Lippard,

> before he came to see the author, the day previous, he had waited upon more than one person, whose eminence in literature was owing to his criticisms—

and how those eminent persons had suffered him to
wait in anterooms and offices, while their very lac-
queys amused themselves by saying—"There's ——
He's drunk again."

All this the day *before* calling at Lippard's office? After
leaving Sartain with borrowed money in his pocket?
If Poe did say all this to Lippard, it is hardly possible
that he said it in July, when he spent all his time drinking, getting himself arrested, and having visions in his
jail cell.

Several other apparent contradictions in the Lippard
article are puzzling. Lippard says that he and another
man, unnamed, went with Poe to the train when he was
leaving for Richmond. But Poe in his letter of July 14th
to Mrs. Clemm says that Burr "saw me off in the cars"
(*Letters,* II, 454), not mentioning Lippard. (Poe's letter to Mrs. Clemm of July 19th, in which Lippard *is*
mentioned in connection with Burr, but not concerning any train departure, obviously relates to the earlier
encounter.)

Most revealing, in my view, is Lippard's failure to
supply any hint that Poe while with him was in a suicidal frame of mind, and in fact shows him as quite
the opposite. Yet in Philadelphia in July, Poe's self-
destructive bent had been all too starkly in evidence, so
much so that it frightened Sartain.

Lastly, the question asked in my text can stand emphasizing. Why was it Lippard, rather than Poe, who
made the rounds of editorial offices soliciting cash? Lippard himself, as he says, was feeling ill to start with,
then got rapidly sicker and had to go home, trying
again the next morning. Poe is not portrayed in the article as in any way sick (he says, "tell them that I am

sick," which seems to say that he really isn't). Why couldn't Poe have made the rounds himself, done his own borrowing? Only one answer appears reasonable: until he could flee the city he had to remain in hiding from his pursuers.

84   *Date of the daguerreotype:* Supposedly, this picture was made at the invitation of the operator himself, William Pratt, who says he was standing in the doorway of his gallery one day when Poe passed by on the sidewalk. The September date for the occasion depends on Pratt's claim—recorded nearly fifty years later, and by a third party, one Thomas Dimmock—that Poe died "three weeks" after the picture was made (Dimmock, 315). In 1854 a copy was made from the original by Pratt himself for Dimmock, who donated it to the Players Club in New York City. (See the photo section.) The only other known copy—it may in fact be the original—is in Butler Library, Columbia University.

84   "He wore a dark"—Weiss, 711. If Poe did not have a moustache when he met this young lady, but grew it back in July–August, she certainly would have noted the fact. In her 1878 article she remarks minutely on his appearance: his face ("not handsome . . . distinguished"), his usual expression ("sad and dreamy"), the shape of his head judged phrenologically (some parts "remarkable"), and his eyes ("his most striking feature," described in detail). At that time, in any case, Susan Talley was the complete disciple, fascinated by every aspect of the man and the writer. A contemporary mention (1850) by an eyewitness of Poe wearing a moustache in Richmond in fall 1849 is in the *Messenger* article by John Daniel: "Mr. Poe's hair was dark, and when we knew him seemed to be slightly sprinkled with grey. He wore a heavy and ill-trimmed

moustache" (180). He adds that Poe "dressed uniformly in good taste . . . the attire of a gentleman."

Seven: What Mrs. Smith Knew

86 *Background of Mrs. Smith:* A prolific writer, busy editor, and minor public personality, Elizabeth Oakes Smith—at times she ran the names together, Oakesmith, as more impressive—was well known in her own time. Her entry in Griswold's *Female Poets of America* is exceeded in length only by that of Maria Brooks, and includes seven pages of biography and critical discussion, longest by far in the volume. Today she is remembered for little more than her link with Poe. Sources for her life are not voluminous, only the brief Twyman biography, treating herself and her husband, her slim *Autobiography,* and mentions in various reference works and in the writings by and about her friends and colleagues. For some portrayal of the New York literary soirees of the day, see the Stern article, and my own volume, *Plumes,* 45–47, 130.

87 "She has very narrowly"—Poe's *Works* (Widdleton), III, 133.

88 "a more absurdly *flat*"—Poe's *Works* (Widdleton), III, 216.

88 "We harbored no"—Smith, *United,* 263.

88 "Not long before his"—Smith, *United,* 268. Published in the March 1857 issue, the article was written only six or seven years after the fact. This magazine itself was owned and edited by the Smiths, husband and wife. In the June 1857 issue she observes: "Since the publication of our critique upon [Poe], we have received several communications from different parts of the country com-

menting upon our remarks, and expressing opinions more or less sympathetic with our article" (633). None of the correspondents took exception to what Mrs. Smith said about Poe's having been beaten.

89 "It is asserted in"—Smith, *Beadle's,* 156. The article is a lengthy one offering a very able discussion of Poe's character as man and poet. On Poe's treatment of her own writings and those of her husband she allows herself to say a little more than in her first article. At her first meeting with the poet, she says, "I was not prepared to be pleased with Mr. Poe. That he had not very much praised *me* in his critique I did not so much care; but I felt he had done my husband an injustice . . . and this had prejudiced me against him." Poe, showing in his manner what she calls a "childlike anxiety," she quotes as saying, "I am afraid my critique on your poems did not please you." In reply, she confesses to having been "half inclined to tell him the real truth, and now I wish I had done so." Instead, she brushed the subject aside with, "I have no right to complain; you doubtless wrote as you thought," to which Poe replied, "I wrote honestly, meaning great praise" (150). This exchange cleared the air and eventually the two became good friends.

90 "That Edgar Poe may"—Smith, *Home Journal,* 14. Parts of this article were lifted from the *Beadle's* piece. The paragraph stating the beating charge is brought in without preamble, and then the topic is as abruptly dropped.

91 "Her most egregious"—Ljunquist and Nickels, 328. This article incorrectly dates the Smith piece in *United States* to 1858 rather than 1857.

91 *Susan Talley on the Smith beating claim:* In a letter to the

New York *Herald* (April 26, 1876), she dismisses the beating charge as "extraordinary and improbable." But she interprets Mrs. Smith as saying that the beating took place *in Richmond,* and she connects it with *Mrs. Shelton's* demand for the return of her letters. The only other public questioning of the beating charge, a vague one, was made by Dr. Snodgrass in his 1867 *Beadle's* article, who calls it "improbable" on the basis of what he personally observed of Poe's condition in the bar and at the hospital (see above, 117).

92 "a divine and a demoniac"—Whitman, *United,* 633. Same for the next quotation. Mrs. Whitman's comments are presented as from "A valued correspondent remarkable for deep, beautiful insight," no name listed. But from other sources it is known that the correspondent was indeed Mrs. Whitman (see Miller, *Helen,* 328). If while reading Mrs. Whitman's half-column of comment the beating charge is kept in mind, her failure to say anything about it grows decidedly conspicuous. The Smith article on Poe, obviously, was stimulating enough to draw from her a long response full of well-considered insight on Poe, but omitting all reference to the sensational question of how he died. This was no mere oversight. It strongly argues acceptance.

92 "of no value"—Miller, *Helen,* 345. In her letter, written to Ingram in October 1875, Mrs. Whitman says, "I have seen Mrs. E. O. Smith's paper on Poe in *Beadle's Monthly,* but I have not seen it for years. I considered it of no value and lost it."

93 "I wonder if you have"—Miller, *Helen,* 413. The letter is dated April 7, 1876.

94 "did not emanate from"—Miller, *Helen,* 450. The letter is dated August 26, 1876.

94 "I regret to say"—Miller, *Helen,* 452. The letter is dated September 12, 1876.

95 "Surely you do not"—Miller, *Helen,* 454. The letter is dated October 19, 1876.

95 "As to EOS, I had the"—Miller, *Helen,* 456. The letter is dated November 2, 1876.

96 *The two phrases:* The first phrase, specifying a "friend" as the one who did the damage to Poe, is in a letter dated April 7, 1876. The second phrase, specifying "brothers" as the assailants, is in a letter written six months later, October 19, 1876. Both phrases as used by Mrs. Whitman were, as she notes, picked up from the newspapers, but in neither case is there any clue as to which papers. In none of her three articles had Mrs. Smith mentioned brothers as being involved, nor had she used such bare terms as "deceived and betrayed" or "betrayed and ruined." The newspapers in question remain unidentified, so there is little further that can be said. But, again, it was not the *who* or the *how* of the matter that upset Mrs. Whitman, it was the charge that Poe had wronged a woman.

In this same regard, one of Poe's other close female friends, Annie Richmond of Lowell, must also be counted among those who declined to question or deny the beating charge as made by Mrs. Smith. Upon reading the *Beadle's* article she promptly wrote to Mrs. Clemm, calling it eagerly to the older woman's attention: "Have you seen a biographical sketch of our darling Eddy by Mrs. Oakes Smith? . . . to be sure it is not *all* you or I would say, but it is such a noble defense against the recent attacks upon him, that I bless her for it & will love her for it as long as I live—I wish I knew her address, & I would write and tell her how grateful I

am & will ever be to her for those kind and just words"
(Quinn and Hart, 63; the letter is dated July 14, 1867).
Not only does Mrs. Richmond, by her silence, accept
the beating charge, she doesn't hesitate to praise the article to Poe's ever-devoted mother-in-law. Apparently
she is not concerned that the woman might be distressed to read that her loved Eddy died from a beating,
which also seems to argue prior acceptance. Unfortunately, there is no record of Mrs. Clemm's reaction—it
may of course be taken for granted that she read the
article (Annie offered to send her a copy).

97   "I saw Poe constantly"—Weiss, 708. Same for the quotations in the next three paragraphs.

97   "He passed from room"—Weiss, 712. Same for the next
two quotations.

98   "a difficulty concerning"—Weiss, *Home,* 197. In her
earlier statement in the New York *Herald* (1876), Talley also spoke of trouble between Elmira and Poe over
letters: "Mr. Poe refused to return certain letters of
hers until she should consent to also give up his own,
which she declined to do, asserting that they had been
destroyed."

99   "Mrs. Shelton, during"—Weiss, *Home,* 197.

99   "There was even a"—Weiss, *Home,* 204. If Susan Talley
didn't know the Shelton family personally—of course,
it is quite possible that she did—as a longtime resident
of Richmond she certainly knew of them. This would
be particularly true in the last months when her literary
idol became engaged to Elmira.

100 *The Royster brothers:* According to Hill's Richmond City
Directory for 1850–52, the three men lived at: 1) Cary
and 22nd Street, then Grace and 21st; 2) 24th between
Broad and Marshall; 3) Grace Street and 27th. Both

James and Alex were employed as clerks at the Virginia Towing Company, based on the Richmond docks (perhaps connected with Alexander Shelton's original carting firm), while George was a clerk for the Dunlop and Moncure Company. Over the years the three also engaged in a fairly large number of commercial transactions, buying and selling property (see Richmond City, Register of Deeds, Hustings and Chancery Court, 1782–1917). Several other Royster men are listed in the directories for those years, and in the U.S. Census of 1850, but I am unsure of the relationships between them and the three brothers.

Not a great deal is on record about the Royster family, which took no part in public affairs or literary matters. In September 1807, James H. Royster, a merchant of Richmond, married Mary G. Bohannon, of Essex County, Virginia (Richmond *Argus,* 19 September 1807). The U.S. Census of 1820 for the city of Richmond lists the couple as having two sons, both under 10, and two daughters, also both under 10. The census doesn't give the names of children, but the boys would have been James B., born 1813, and Alexander, born 1816 (Census of 1850). The girls were Elmira, born 1810, and Lucy, born 1815. The third son, George, born late 1820 or early 1821, came too late for the 1820 census. The elder Royster died in May 1833 of unspecified causes while in North Carolina (Richmond *Whig,* 24 May 1833). His widow, Mary G. Royster, is listed in the 1840 census as head of a household which included one male under 30, which would be George. For the Poe interlude of 1849 the widow was still alive but apparently took no part in it, except perhaps behind the scenes. She died at age 81 in 1858 at the home of her son James (Moore, *Henrico,* 356; Richmond *Times-Dispatch,* 16 February 1858).

All three of the Royster boys married and raised children. In 1837 James married Jane Henshaw and fathered at least two sons. In 1840 Alexander married Susan (last name not available), and fathered two sons and a daughter. In 1843 George married Mary (last name not available), and lived to 1897, when he died of heart trouble. Both Royster girls were also married, Elmira as detailed in the text, and Lucy to George Trible in 1833 (Moore, *Henrico,* 241, 245, 276, 361; records of Shockoe Hill Cemetery; Census of 1850).

100 *Mrs. Smith's source:* The closest she came to saying anything specific about sources, additional to her three articles, is a paragraph in a private letter to Ingram. But it only serves to further tantalize: "You say truly Poe was murdered. When the memory of this delicate, sensitive child of genius with his weird unearthly eyes rises to my mind's eye coupled with the last days of horror and inhumanity, I am distressed beyond measure; but alas! how like a tragedy life becomes when we have looked behind the scenes!" (letter of June 8, 1875, original at the University of Virginia). Ingram, apparently, was not impressed by Mrs. Smith's articles, or by that mention of "the last days of horror," for he ignored Mrs. Smith's beating charge and chose the "cooping" theory as his solution. Rather glaring is his not bothering to comment on the beating charge, for him an unusual oversight.

100 *Mrs. Smith's Richmond contacts:* Her connection with the prominent White family may have begun when Thomas White published in his *Messenger* her best-known poem, *The Sinless Child* (1842). However it happened,

they became close, to the point where Mrs. Smith was asked to receive Lizzie White as a guest in her home in New York for a lengthy stay, seemingly to provide the young lady with a wider field. This she did, soon being convinced of the old rumors that Lizzie and Poe would have married had it not been for the interference of Mrs. Clemm on behalf of her own daughter, Virginia. (See the several letters of Mrs. Smith to Ingram in 1875, originals at the University of Virginia.) Through the Whites, Mrs. Smith's further contact with Richmond circles is assured.

There were also, of course, her professional links as a journalist with the various Richmond editors, in particular J. R. Thompson of the *Messenger,* and J. M. Daniel of the *Examiner.* Exactly who it was in Richmond— I think it *must* have been someone in Richmond—who informed Mrs. Smith as to the part taken by the Shelton brothers in Poe's death I am unable to say. At a guess I would choose Daniel, who had an article in the *Messenger* soon after Poe's death in which he both praises and damns him. No other American writer, he declares, had half the chance to be remembered, but "his irregularities, his caprices, his total disregard for everything and [every]body, save for the fancy in his head, prevented him from doing well in the world. . . . He believed in nobody, and cared for nobody" (180). He also says that the truth about Poe's break with his foster-father "throws . . . a very ugly light upon Poe's character," but declines to be more specific.

102 *Poe and Thompson:* The acquaintance of these two in the summer and fall of 1849 in Richmond is well established, as is the fact that Poe made the *Messenger* office "his headquarters." See the standard biographies.

102 "dreamy abstraction"—Thompson, *Genius,* 39.

102 "impossible to consider"—Thompson, *Genius,* 37.

102 "He had extraordinary"—Thompson, *Genius,* 40.

103 "some hard things of "—Thompson, *Genius,* 57 (an appendix added later to the lecture). Same for the next quotation.

103 "died, indeed, of delirium"—Quinn, 569.

103 "an attack of delirium"—Miller, *Helen,* 41. Mrs. Mowatt's letter, a long one, is quoted in Mrs. Whitman to Ingram, February 27, 1874, given as having been received in 1859.

103 "seized by the lawless"—Thompson, *Genius,* 42.

Eight: Suddenly a Tapping

106 *Poe's departure from Elmira:* Dr. Carter says Poe reached his office that night at about nine-thirty. Measuring the distance between Elmira's house and Carter's office, I judge that he left Elmira some twenty minutes before that. She doesn't state in her letter to Mrs. Clemm that she felt Poe's forehead. But simply feeling his pulse, which she did do, would not have revealed a definite fever. Neither does she say that she suggested to Poe a postponement of the trip, or that he mentioned the Loud appointment to her, or that he brushed aside his feeling ill. But these things are all quite plainly implicit in what she did write in her letter of October 9th, and in the known situation (see above, 132, for the relevant passage in Elmira's letter). It was the appointment with Mrs. Loud in Philadelphia, more than anything, I feel, that kept him to his schedule, even when feeling physically weak. I am thus minute and particular at the outset of this chapter in order to demonstrate something of my procedure in analysis and interpretation of sources.

108 "I had not seen Poe"—Carter, 565. The title of this article, "Edgar Poe's Last Night in Richmond," is misleading. Of fair length at 2,500 words, hardly 10 percent of it deals with that last night, and nothing else in it bears on the present study. Carter does not say that Poe, in taking the sword-cane, left his own; in fact he doesn't refer at all to Poe as carrying a cane. But that Poe customarily did so is attested by Susan Talley. "I vividly recall him as he appeared on his visits to us. He always carried a cane . . ." (Weiss, 711). Because Poe took the cane with him on leaving the office, Carter, as he says, "inferred that he expected to return shortly," that is, come back in order to return the borrowed cane, but he didn't. My suggestion as to why Poe took the sword-cane—a deliberate act, surely—is the only one that makes any sense, I strongly feel. For more on the cane see three notes down.

109 "They wept and pleaded"—Dietz, 40.

109 *The sword-cane:* A curious error concerning this weapon has lurked undetected in Poe biography for a long time. In his 1909 volume Woodberry states that Poe, when found in Baltimore, was still clutching the cane: "It is a trifling but interesting detail that the Malacca cane had stuck to him through all his adventures" (II, 343). For this assertion he offers no evidence, an obvious gap which didn't prevent Hervey Allen from showing the rescued poet as "still grasping Dr. Carter's cane" (673), as also Quinn who has Poe "still grasping the cane of Dr. Carter" (639). Even the ever-wary Mabbott says that Poe when found "had the Malacca cane; would lawless fellows have failed to purloin so salable an object?" (569), a thought echoed as late as 1987 (Bandy, "Myth," 26). Silverman is more careful. He agrees that Poe took the cane from the doctor's office but he allows it just to disappear from his text (433).

In neither of his two articles, of course, does Snodgrass say anything about Poe grasping a cane when found, nor is it elsewhere asserted in contemporary sources. What it was that led Woodberry to his mistaken conclusion I cannot imagine, unless it was a deduction from something said by Carter in his article. The personal effects that Poe left in storage at the Swan, Carter explains, were eventually retrieved by the MacKenzies, "and through the same source I received my cane" (566). To me, this only means that the cane turned up among Poe's other things stored at the Swan, thus had been forgotten by him and left in his room.

109 *Poe at Sadler's Restaurant:* Carter, 565–66, Whitty, lxxxiii, Weiss, 714. Whitty's information came directly from Judge Robert Hughes of Richmond, who knew both Sadler and J. M. Blakey of the Swan. It is possible that Hughes was present at Sadler's that night, but on this Whitty is unclear.

110 *The boat for Baltimore:* Exactly what steamer Poe took when leaving Richmond on the morning of September 27th has been much argued, to no conclusion (see Harrison, 327, Woodberry, II, 342, Phillips, 1494, and, especially, Quinn, 755–56. Silverman, 433, ignores the point, simply stating that Poe left "on the 4 A.M. steamer," echoing Woodberry). The possibilities are several, but I am convinced that he went by the United States Line, whose schedule was as I give it. See the regular advertisements for this line in the Richmond papers.

111 *Train departures for Philadelphia:* Here I follow Quinn, 637–38, whose brother was General Passenger Agent for the Pennsylvania Railroad (755).

113 "Early one Monday"—Sartain, "Reminiscences," 413.

Same for the succeeding quotations relating to this incident.

114 "a woman trouble"—Sartain, "Reminiscences," 413, also in Sartain, *Old Man,* 207. The point deserves dwelling on. If, for instance, Poe did use such a phrase to Sartain in July 1849, *what* could it have meant? Really, the only possibility open is trouble over some new, unsuspected, and still unknown woman encountered in Philadelphia after he reached there on June 30th. Personally, I think that the number of Poe women already on hand is quite sufficient without ringing in another, this one unnamed and unidentified!

115 "mental overstrain"—Sartain, "Last Days," in Tuerk, 22. The phrase is used to describe Poe when he first entered Sartain's office on Sansom Street that morning: "I saw at a glance that he was suffering from mental overstrain, and I assured him of shelter."

115 "until he was absolutely"—Sartain, "Last Days," in Tuerk, 22.

115 *The secondhand clothes:* These are described here according to the lists given by Snodgrass in his two articles. That Poe discarded his own clothes I deduce from the fact that they didn't turn up in his trunk, and no sign of them ever surfaced. Probably they were left at the secondhand store in part payment, and went on display for purchase as soon as he left. Sartain's home and office at 728 Sansom Street, between 7th and 8th, was only a block from the city's Market Street clothing district where some dozen large stores offered every type of apparel, wholesale, retail, and secondhand (see newspaper ads of the day).

116 *Possible blow to the head of Poe:* Courtney, 114. This author, like so many who have chosen to set aside the clear evidence of Poe's intoxication at the end—really irrefu-

table—offers this conclusion: "It is appealing to pos-
tulate that, like many who are seen in emergency rooms
today, he suffered the fate of being mistaken for a common drunk. Poe's condition could easily have been the
result of intracerebral trauma, and his lucid interval, if
Moran's story can be relied upon, would even lend support to the diagnosis of epidural hematoma." That is
the opinion of a qualified physician, and as such deserves a hearing. However, Dr. Courtney seems not to
have been very conversant with Poe sources, for he has
the poet doing something he never did, delivering "nu-
merous lectures in which he warned against the sin of
alcohol." He also has Poe regularly using opium, an old
error now quite discredited. Also, of course, Dr. Moran
said nothing about any supposed "lucid interval." In his
letter to Mrs. Clemm (November 1849), Moran says
only that he was able to induce "tranquility" in the patient but that his talk was never more than "incoherent
and unsatisfactory."

117 "I am positive that"—Snodgrass, *Beadle's*, 285. His first
article says nothing about possible injuries.

117 "ripped seams . . . soiled"—Snodgrass, *Beadle's*, 284.

118 *Forcing Poe to drink:* Certainly, as part of their plan, the
brothers would have intended that the news of Poe's apparent debauch should reach the Baltimore papers, inevitably to be copied by papers in Richmond, as had
happened with all the stories about Poe's taking the
pledge. In addition, once back in Richmond they would
probably have arranged to tip off a number of reporters and editors anonymously. What forestalled this was
something they never anticipated, his death.

120 *Poe in the hospital:* My detailed picture of this, including
the final moments, comes entirely from a close reading

of Dr. Moran's letter to Mrs. Clemm. I refrain from attempting to state what was, or might have been the precise or immediate physical cause of his expiring as he did. There simply is not enough medical evidence at hand.

121 "he had a wife in Richmond"—Moran, in Quinn and Hart, 33. This claim by Poe came in the midst of his rambling replies to the doctor's gentle questioning about possible relatives. That the remark was clearly stated by the patient and clearly understood by the doctor is indicated by Moran's taking the trouble to check ("which, I have since learned, was not the case"). He doesn't say when or how he did the checking, but apparently it was in direct correspondence with Elmira, with whom he exchanged several letters soon after Poe's death (*Defense,* 12).

121 "blow out his brains"—Moran, in Quinn and Hart, 33. When Poe uttered these despairing words, I judge, he'd at last become fully aware of his situation. It was then that he abandoned hope, his crushed spirit hastening, if it did not cause, his death, which came, it is known from Neilson's letter, as a sudden reversal (see two notes down).

121 "Reynolds"—The name is a fairly common one, and it occurs a number of times in Poe's career, none with any close personal ties. Speculation so far on the point has been pretty far-fetched, and even if true not significant. The 1987 article by Bandy provides a brief overview of the question. Bandy's own conclusion is that Poe's dying outcry was, not "Reynolds!" but the name of his cousin, "Herring!" But even a doctor or nurse with a tin ear could hardly confuse those two names, especially when heard shouted over and over through the night

in the silent hospital ward! Moran's report of the name
was made in his early letter to Mrs. Clemm. More interesting to me is the presence at the polls that day of
Henry Reynolds, a carpenter by profession, as an election judge (Baltimore *Sun,* 3 October 1849, p. 1, col. 4,
under heading "The Polls and the Judges," first reported by Stern in his *Saturday Review* article). Was the
judge's name perhaps repeatedly spoken aloud in the
crowded room, at last penetrating Poe's stupor and
arousing vague associations now untraceable? There we
will leave the topic, judging it only fitting that not
everything about so convoluted a personality can be
explained.

123 "I was never so shocked"—Quinn and Hart, 30. He
made two visits but may not have actually seen Poe.

Added Note to Chapter Eight

Tentatively, I think that Joseph Walker himself may
deserve closer scrutiny than has been given him. The
fact that he had earlier worked for Snodgrass as a typesetter on the *Baltimore Saturday Visitor* was noted by
Snodgrass (*Beadle's,* 1867). The further relevant fact
that he had once been employed in the same capacity
on the Baltimore *Sun,* perhaps even in 1849, was first
reported by Spencer (*Herald,* 1881), and has since been
regularly noted by biographers, though without comment. Yet it does seem a curious circumstance: the one
man in the milling crowd of voters at Gunner's Hall to
take notice of the helpless Poe proves to be linked not
only with Snodgrass, but with the city's leading newspaper. The coincidence, once admitted, raises some interesting questions.

For instance, in Walker's note the phrase "who goes under the cognomen of Edgar A. Poe" seems a quite a stilted way of putting the fact, even confusing ("whose name is," or "who calls himself" would be ordinary usage). Does it mean that Poe *told* Walker his name? If so, would a man in Poe's disoriented state really have specified his middle initial? Perhaps Walker read the name on something he found in Poe's pocket, which fits better with the peculiar wording, "goes under." Yet Poe *was* able to speak, clearly pronouncing Snodgrass' name ("he says he is acquainted with you").

If Poe was so far gone as to be in need of *immediate* assistance, as the note claims—a man in "great distress"—why did Walker leave him to his fate after sending the note? He couldn't have been certain that it would reach its target, or that, if it did, the needed help would be timely. Did Walker recognize the name as that of the famous writer? He should have, yet his wording seems to say that he didn't. If not, then surely he became aware of the fact when his own paper, the *Sun,* five days later announced Poe's death—Walker might even have been the compositor who set the story in type! Yet he apparently left on record not the slightest hint of his own important role in the historic event. His accidental death by drowning, while swimming in "the Spring Gardens," was first reported by Spencer (*Herald,* 1881), no year or other circumstances supplied.

In Matchett's Baltimore Directory for 1853 four Joseph Walkers are listed, one being Joseph W., a printer (the listings for 1849–52 give several Joseph Walkers, none printers). The home address given is 4 Stirling Street. If this was Walker's residence in 1849 then a curious situation is uncovered, for Stirling Street was not located in the Fourth Ward. It was a short, three-block stretch between West Eager Street and Monument Street, well to the north of Gunner's Hall, in the Sixth Ward. In that case, his going to Ryan's polls on election day could not have been for the purpose of casting a vote—a possibility giving considerable reason for pause. If in 1849 he in fact was a Fourth Ward resident, then of course his presence there had a legitimate basis, though it doesn't lessen the coincidence of *his* being the one to offer help. (In 1849 a *teacher* named Joseph W. Walker lived at 101 South Exeter Street, which was in the Fourth Ward not far from Gunner's Hall. But this same man appears in the 1853 *Directory* at the same address, along with Joseph W. Walker, the printer, on Stirling Street.)

I have no firm conclusion to offer on all this, only what I may term a dim suspicion or surmise, hardly strong enough for pursuing, if pursuit were possible. Could Joseph Walker in some unsuspecting way have been used by the Royster brothers in their plan to inform the Baltimore newspapers about Poe's supposed fall into renewed debauchery? Did Walker, when he returned to work that day (October 3rd was a Wednesday), or the next day, tell the *Sun* editor about his unpleasant encounter with the famous poet? If so, the editor for some reason sat on the story, defeating the Roysters' evident design: during the three full days Poe spent in the hospital, 4–6 October, the paper carried nothing on him. Confirmation of his death—an unexpected outcome, in fact shocking, in the view of Neilson Poe—on Sunday, October 7th, must have reached the *Sun* office within a very few hours for the story to have been included in Monday morning's paper, arguing ready contact.

Epilogue: Exit the Widow

124 "the horrible truth"—Woodberry, *Century,* 552. Quotations in the next three paragraphs are from this same letter.

125 "would beg to be excused"—Elmira Shelton to George Eveleth, December 22, 1852, copy by Eveleth at the University of Virginia. In this short note of reply to Eveleth she even avoids naming Poe, referring to him as "the person in question." She also mentions receiving a request for financial help from Mrs. Clemm, and says, "I intend as soon as opportunity affords to render her some assistance." Her contact with Poe's relative was quickly ended, however, and in 1859 Mrs. Clemm put her resentment of the neglect in a letter: "I have not heard from Mrs. Shelton for a long time . . . she has not been the friend to me that you have, and she is rich, too, but I will not blame her, for she I suppose is entirely estranged from me" (quoted in Harrison, "Romance," 448). Her extreme reticence concerning Poe was also noted in her *Whig* obituary: "So intimate were her connections with him that his life and in-most thoughts must have been as an open book to her . . . when death had once put an irrevocable seal upon his lips her own were closed, too, upon those pages of his existence."

125 *Elmira as Poe's inspiration:* A number of sources record her denial that she had inspired any of Poe's verse (Dietz, 43, for instance). The only exception that I have found is the Alfriend article of 1901. "Mrs. Shelton also told me," writes Alfriend, "that Poe informed her over and over again that she was the 'Lost Lenore' of The Raven; she also said that Poe told her that she inspired his poem, 'Annabel Lee'" (490). The contradiction, I am satisfied, is only what might be expected from a woman of more advanced age, giving way in private to a desire to have the truth as she saw it on record. That Elmira was known and talked of in Richmond in later years as the authentic inspiration of *The Raven* is attested by one of Poe's more competent early biographers, James Harrison of Richmond. He referred once to Elmira as "a lady whom the author, living in the same town with her in 1871–76, used to hear familiarly called 'Poe's Lenore'" (Harrison, 313).

125 "Poe's first and last love"—Richmond *Whig,* page one obituary, February 12, 1888. The story of the youthful love is given, as is the later engagement, but with an air of uncertainty. During his stay in Richmond in 1849, said the paper, Poe, "renewed his attentions to Mrs. Shelton, and it was rumored that an engagement existed between them. Mrs. Shelton is said to have denied this, but as she went into mourning after his death, it is to be presumed that this was incorrect." Whether Elmira really did go into mourning at Poe's death—she denied it to Valentine rather emphatically—is an interesting possibility. Susan Talley, for one, seems to say that she personally *saw* Elmira dressed in appropriate black at the time: "On his death she appeared in public attired in deepest widow's weeds" (Weiss, *Home,* 201). Note the "in public." If Elmira did put on mourning it would hardly be surprising, considering how she felt that tragic October. To Mrs. Clemm she confessed that to her Poe had been "the *dearest object* on earth," and to Dr. Moran some days or weeks later she wrote of him as having been "more to me than any other living being" (Moran, *Defense,* 12). Of course, her wearing of mourning dress would have preceded her learning of her

brothers' involvement. This, I estimate on the basis of her letter to Moran, was no more than a week or two after Poe's death.

126 "There are many others"—From the original letter, dated November 5, 1874, at the Valentine Museum, Richmond.

126 "before it was rumored"—Ingram, "Memoir" (in the Lovell edition of Poe's *Poems*), 75.

126 "I heard on Saturday"—From the original letter at the Valentine Museum, Richmond. Why did she admit to "a partial understanding"? Again, I think it was her vanity catching up with her, in addition to nostalgia, as old age approached. Some sort of special link with her old love, the famous poet, she *did* wish to preserve as the years sped by. Very human and understandable, I feel.

127 "I did not put on a"—The Valentine interview, from the original manuscript at the Valentine Museum, Richmond.

128 "does not appear to"—Ingram, 425.

128 "the strength of the"—Moran, *Defense,* 34. Same for the next quotation in this paragraph.

128 "the venerable lady"—Moran, *Defense,* 35. This later contact of Dr. Moran with the elderly Mrs. Shelton has been overlooked, as has the fact that his little book of 1885 is dedicated to her. When the book appeared, of course, she was still living, but there is no record of her reaction to it. "The interview," adds Moran feelingly, "I shall never forget. Our sympathies were in unison, and I am not ashamed to confess that it was with difficulty that [my] tears were restrained." He says that Elmira was in feeble health, but that "her face indicates a peaceful mind and a joyous hope of the rest beyond"

(36). This agrees with what Elmira herself said about her health in a letter of June 1880, a couple of years before Moran saw her: "My health is extremely delicate, and I have been very sick recently." The letter was written to John Ingram, thanking him for a copy of his Poe biography, recently published. "I am reading it with deep interest," she says, "and find much in it which revives many *sad* remembrances, as well as *very pleasant* ones" (original at the University of Virginia).

129 "I write to you to"— Quoted in Moran, *Defense,* 12, from the original. Just when and how Elmira learned the truth of her brothers' involvement must for now be left to the imagination. Perhaps it was a result of a confession to her by one of the three, possibly Alexander, whose house on Grace Street she gave as a mailing address two days after hearing of Poe's death (see above, 134).

Acknowledgments

The kindness and accommodating spirit of many librarians and archivists did much to facilitate the lengthy research effort underlying this book. To the efficient staffs of the following institutions go my heartfelt thanks:

Memorial Library, University of Wisconsin; the Library and Archives of the Wisconsin Historical Society, Madison; the Library of Virginia, Richmond; The Virginia Historical Society, Richmond; The Poe Shrine and Museum, Richmond; The Valentine Museum, Richmond; Alderman Library, University of Virginia; The Maryland Historical Society, Baltimore; The Enoch Pratt Free Library, Baltimore; Lilly Library, Indiana University; Ransom Research Center, University of Texas at Austin; the Graduate Library, University of Michigan; Barnard College; Fales Library, New York University; the Hampden-Booth Theatre Library, The Players Club; The New York Public Library at 42nd Street; The New-York Historical Society; Dixon Homestead Library, Dumont, New

Jersey; the Boston Public Library; Houghton Library, Harvard University; Stirling Library, Yale University; the Monroe (Wisconsin) Public Library.

No less is my debt to the many able and dedicated Poe scholars who preceded me. Without their pioneering efforts in researching the life of the poet, and the stimulus of their work and opinions, my own task would have been infinitely more difficult. My obligations to them may be read in the Bibliography and the Notes.

For various sorts of timely aid, grateful thanks go to my patient wife Dorothy, and to my sons: John C. Walsh, George Mason University; Timothy A. Walsh, University of Wisconsin; Matthew O. Walsh, Dallas, Texas; and also, and especially, to my daughter, Ann (Mrs. William Marriott), Wayland, Massachusetts.

Selected Bibliography

Abbreviations are used where clear in themselves: EAP = Edgar Allan Poe, etc. Page numbers for periodicals are supplied in the Notes, so are not given here. Place of publication unless otherwise stated is New York City.

Alfriend, E. "Unpublished Recollections of EAP." *Literary Era* (August 1901).

Allen, H. *Israfel: The Life and Times of EAP.* Farrar, 1934.

————, and Mabbott, T. *Poe's Brother.* Doran, 1926.

Baird, W. "EAP." *Southern Magazine* (August 1874).

Bandy, W. "The Date of Poe's Burial." *Poe Studies* (December 1971).

————. "Two Notes on Poe's Death." *Poe Studies* (December 1981).

————. "Dr. Moran and the Poe-Reynolds Myth." In Fisher, *Myth.*

Benitez, R. "A 39-Year-Old Man with Mental Status Change." *Maryland Medical Journal* (September 1996).

Benton, R. "Friends and Enemies: Women in the Life of EAP." In Fisher, *Myth*.

Bramsback, B. "The Final Illness and Death of EAP." *Studia Philologica* [Stockholm] 62 (1970).

Burr, C. "Character of EAP." *Nineteenth Century* (February 1852).

Carlson, E. *A Companion to Poe Studies*. Westport, Conn.: Greenwood Press, 1996.

Carter, J. "Edgar Poe's Last Night in Richmond." *Lippincott's* (November 1902).

Clark, G. "Two Unnoticed Recollections of Poe's Funeral." *Poe Newsletter* (June 1970).

Courtney, J. "Addiction and EAP." *Resident and Staff Physician* (January 1971).

Daniel, J. "EAP." *Southern Literary Messenger* (March 1850).

Didier, E. *Life and Poems of EAP*. Widdleton, 1877.

———. *The Poe Cult and Other Papers*. Broadway, 1909.

Dietz, F. "Poe's First and Final Love." *Southern Literary Messenger* (March 1943).

Dimmock, T. "Notes on Poe." *Century* (June 1895).

Dowdey, C. "Poe's Last Visit to Richmond." *American Heritage* (April 1956).

Eaves, T. "Poe's Last Visit to Philadelphia." *American Literature* (March 1954).

Fairfield, F. "A Mad Man of Letters." *Scribner's* (October 1875).

Fisher, B. *Myth and Reality: The Mysterious Mr. Poe*. Baltimore: EAP Society, 1987.

———. *Poe and His Times*. Baltimore: EAP Society, 1990.

Gill, W. *The Life of EAP*. Dillingham, 1877.

Graves, C. "Landmarks of Poe in Richmond." *Century* (April 1904).

Griswold, R. *The Female Poets of America.* Carey and Hart, 1848.

———. "EAP." *International Miscellany* (June 1850).

Groves, B. "Death of Poe: The Case for Hypoglycemia." *Artes Liberales* 5 (1979).

Harrison, J. *Life of EAP.* 1903. Reprint. Haskell House, 1970.

———. "The Romance of Poe and Mrs. Whitman." *Century* (January 1909).

Hill, J. "The Diabetic Mr. Poe." *Poe Newsletter* (October 1968).

Hubbell, J. "Chauncey Burr." *PMLA* (September 1954).

Ingram, J. "Memoir of EAP." In *Poems of EAP.* Widdleton, 1874.

———. "Unpublished Correspondence of EAP." *Appleton's Journal* (May 1878).

———. *EAP: His Life, Letters and Opinions.* 1880. Reprint. AMS Press, 1965.

Lippard, G. "EAP." *Sunday Mercury* [Philadelphia] (1853). Reprinted in Eaves.

Ljunquist, K., and Nickels, C. "Elizabeth Oakes Smith on Poe: A Chapter in the Recovery of His 19th Century Reputation." In Fisher, *Times.*

McElroy, M. "Poe's Last Partner." *Papers on Language and Literature* (Summer 1971).

Mabbott, T. *Annals of EAP.* In *Collected Works of EAP* (volume 1, *Poems*). Cambridge: Harvard University Press, 1969.

Meyers, J. *EAP: His Life and Legacy.* Scribner's, 1992.

Miller, J. *Building Poe Biography.* Baton Rouge: Louisiana State University Press, 1977.

———. *Poe's Helen Remembers.* Charlottesville: University Press of Virginia, 1979.

Moore, J. S. *Annals and History of Henrico Parish, Diocese of Virginia,* 1904. Reprint. Baltimore: Genealogical Publishing Co., 1979.

Moore, R. "A Note on Poe and the Sons of Temperance." *American Literature* (November 1958).

Moran, J. "Official Memoranda of the Death of EAP." New York *Herald,* 28 October 1875.

———. *A Defense of EAP.* Boogher, 1885.

Moss, S. *Poe's Major Crisis.* Durham: Duke University Press, 1970.

Phillips, M. *EAP, The Man.* Philadelphia: Winston, 1926.

Poe, E. A. *The Letters of EAP.* Edited by J. W. Ostrom. Reprint. Gordian Press, 1966.

Quinn, A. H. *EAP: A Critical Biography.* 1941. Reprint. Lanham, Md.: Cooper Square, 1966.

———, and Hart, R. *Poe Letters and Documents in the Enoch Pratt Free Library.* Baltimore: Scholarly Reprints, 1941.

Rein, D. "Poe and Mrs. Shelton." *American Literature* (June 1956).

———. "Poe and Elmira." In *EAP: The Inner Pattern.* Philosophical Library, 1960.

Robertson, J. *EAP: A Study.* Brough, 1921.

Sartain, J. "Reminiscences of EAP." *Lippincott's* (March 1889).

———. "Poe in Philadelphia." *The Press* [Philadelphia], 19 June 1892.

———. "Poe's Last Days." Boston *Evening Transcript,* 25 February 1893. Reprinted in Tuerk.

———. *The Reminiscences of a Very Old Man.* Appleton, 1899.

Silverman, K. *EAP: Mournful and Never-Ending Remembrance.* HarperCollins, 1991.

Smith, E. O. "EAP." *United States Magazine* (March 1857).

————. "Autobiographic Notes: EAP." *Beadle's Monthly* (February 1867).

————. "Reminiscences." *Baldwin's Monthly* (September 1874).

————. "Recollections of Poe." *Home Journal,* 15 May 1876.

————. *Selections from the Autobiography of Elizabeth Oakes Smith.* Edited by M. Wyman. Lewiston, Maine, 1924.

Snodgrass, J. "Death and Burial of EAP." *Life Illustrated* (N.Y.), 15 May 1856. Reprinted in Thomas and Jackson, *Log,* 844–45.

————. "The Facts of Poe's Death and Burial." *Beadle's Monthly* (March 1867).

Spencer, E. "The Memory of Poe." New York *Herald,* 27 March 1881.

Stern, M. "House of Expanding Doors." *New York History* 23 (1942).

Stern, P. "The Strange Death of EAP." *Saturday Review of Literature,* 15 October 1949.

Stoddard, R. H. "Edgar Allan Poe." *Harper's* (September 1872).

Thomas, D., and Jackson, D. *The Poe Log: A Documentary Life of EAP.* Boston: G. K. Hall, 1987.

Thompson, J. R. *The Genius and Character of EAP.* Edited by Whitty and Rindfleisch. Privately printed, 1929.

Ticknor, C. *Poe's Helen.* Scribner's, 1916.

Tuerk, R. "John Sartain and EAP." *Poe Studies* (December 1971).

Walsh, J. *Poe the Detective: The Curious Circumstances Behind The Mystery of Marie Roget.* New Brunswick, N.J.: Rutgers University Press, 1969.

————. *Plumes in the Dust: The Love Affair of EAP and Fanny Osgood.* Chicago: Nelson Hall, 1981.

Weiss, S. A. "Last Days of EAP." *Scribner's* (March 1878).

———. *The Home Life of Poe.* Broadway, 1907.

Whitty, J. "Memoir of Poe." In *Poems of Poe.* Boston: Houghton, 1911.

Wilkinson, A. "John Moncure Daniel." *Richmond College Historical Papers,* 15 June 1915.

Woodberry, G. "The Poe-Chivers Papers." *Century* (February 1903).

———. *Life of EAP.* Boston: Houghton, 1909.

Wyman, M. *Two American Pioneers: Seba Smith and Elizabeth Oakes Smith.* Columbia University Press, 1927.

Index

About the Author

J O H N E V A N G E L I S T W A L S H is the author of more than a dozen books of history and biography, all based on original research. As historian he treats such topics as the invention of the airplane, the search for St. Peter's body in Rome, the great Piltdown fraud, and the Shroud of Turin. As biographer he has probed the lives and careers of such literary figures as Robert Frost and Emily Dickinson. His investigation of the legendary romance between Abraham Lincoln and Ann Rutledge, *The Shadows Rise,* was a finalist for the annual Lincoln Prize of Gettysburg College. His *Poe the Detective: The Curious Circumstances Behind The Mystery of Marie Roget,* was awarded an Edgar by the Mystery Writers of America. Two of his books were condensed in *Reader's Digest: One Day At Kitty Hawk,* and *Night On Fire* (about the epic battle between John Paul Jones' *Bonhomme Richard* and the British *Serapis*). Mr. Walsh is married, and has four grown children and three grandchildren. He lives with his wife Dorothy in Monroe, Wisconsin.